BRIGHT NOTES

JOSEPH ANDREWS BY HENRY FIELDING

Intelligent Education

Nashville, Tennessee

BRIGHT NOTES: Joseph Andrews
www.BrightNotes.com

No part of this publication may be used or reproduced in any manner whatsoever without written permission, except in the case of brief quotations in critical articles and reviews. For permissions, contact Influence Publishers http://www.influencepublishers.com.

ISBN: 978-1-645421-88-7 (Paperback)
ISBN: 978-1-645421-89-4 (eBook)

Published in accordance with the U.S. Copyright Office Orphan Works and Mass Digitization report of the register of copyrights, June 2015.

Originally published by Monarch Press.
Joseph E. Grennen, 1965
2020 Edition published by Influence Publishers.

Interior design by Lapiz Digital Services. Cover Design by Thinkpen Designs.

Printed in the United States of America.

Library of Congress Cataloging-in-Publication Data forthcoming.
Names: Intelligent Education
Title: BRIGHT NOTES: Joseph Andrews
Subject: STU004000 STUDY AIDS / Book Notes

CONTENTS

1)	Introduction to Henry Fielding	1
2)	Brief Summary	5
3)	Textual Analysis	10
	Book I	10
	Book II	38
	Book III	64
	Book IV	82
4)	Character Analyses	99
5)	Critical Commentary	106
6)	Essay Questions and Answers	110
7)	Subject Bibliography and Guide to Research Papers	114

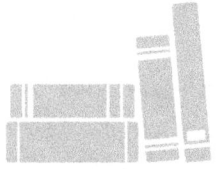

INTRODUCTION TO HENRY FIELDING

EARLY LIFE

Henry Fielding was born in 1707 at Sharpham Park in Somersetshire, and spent his boyhood on a farm at East Stour in Dorsetshire. His father, Edmund Fielding, was an army officer who later rose to the rank of General; his mother, the daughter of Sir Henry Gould, died when Fielding was eleven. For the next few years he attended Eton, where he accumulated an impressive knowledge of the classics (his father, meanwhile, having remarried and become estranged from the Goulds, so that Henry's precise relationship with him is uncertain). At the age of nineteen, we find Fielding in London, where, for the next several years, he supported himself by writing for the theater, his first play, *Love in Several Masques* (a rather artificial comedy of manners), being produced in 1728, when he was 21. For a brief period (1728-29) he studied at the University of Leyden, but returned to London to resume his career in the theater. By 1737, when the Theatrical Licensing Act was passed, effectively ending his dramatic career, he had produced a number of plays, of which *The Author's Farce*, *Rape Upon Rape*, and two translations of Moliere's dramas, *The Miser*, and *The Mock Doctor* are significant. His dramatic adaptation of Cervantes' *Don Quixote* is interesting as showing the continuing hold that book had on him, as witnessed also by the references in *Joseph Andrews* (and on the title page - "written in imitation of the manner of Cervantes").

Fielding married Charlotte Cradock in 1734, by whom he had two daughters, the eldest of which died in 1742, not long after the publication of *Joseph Andrews*. His wife, with whom he was deeply in love, died in 1744. Fielding's vocal opposition to the Walpole government (which had been mainly responsible for the Licensing Act) led to his editing of the Champion, in which his essays appeared most frequently over the pseudonym of Hercules Vinegar. Under the pressure of requiring steady gainful employment, Fielding, for three years, read law and was called to the Bar in 1740, thereafter travelling the Western Circuit.

PAMELA TO JOSEPH ANDREWS

The years of his life which most nearly concern us here are the years 1740 - 42. In November of 1740, Samuel Richardson published his *Pamela: Or Virtue Rewarded*, the story of a young servant girl, who, upon the death of her mistress, was continually assailed by her young master, Mr. Booby, with whom she actually fell in love, but whose importunities she had to reject, ostensibly (and apparently this was Richardson's serious intention) for the preservation of her virtue until, by some stroke of fortune, she might become his wife. To a man of Fielding's sensibility, however, it was inviting to read the entire affair as the artful manipulation of her charms by a calculating and socially ambitious young woman. In *Shamela* (1741), Fielding masterfully parodied the interminable letter-writing and involved ratiocination of Richardson's epistolary novel.

In *Joseph Andrews* (1742), however, he made only glancing references to *Pamela*, preferring instead to make of an ironic reversal of Richardson's situation (here, a chaste young man being seduced by a lustful female) a plot which would be the basis for an extended comic treatment of human vanity and affectation.

PREFACE TO JOSEPH ANDREWS

In the preface to *Joseph Andrews*, Fielding makes it clear that he is writing a "comic **epic** poem in prose," **burlesque** treatment sometimes being admitted in the **diction** but never in the sentiments of his work. He intends to treat not the "monstrous" but the ridiculous," mainly because "a more rational and useful pleasure arises to us from it." The ridiculous arises from vanity and affectation, and these will be the sources of his characterizations, everything in the final analysis being copied from "the book of nature," even though their immediate source is to be found in his own observation and experience.

LATER LIFE

In 1743 Fielding published Jonathan Wild; in 1747 he married Mary Daniel (by whom he had five children); in 1748 he had the satisfaction of being made magistrate for Middlesex. The year 1749, however, saw the publication of his great triumph, *The History of Tom Jones, A Foundling*. This sprawling **epic** of eighteenth-century life and manners has long stood the test of time as one of the greatest, if not the greatest, of English comic novels. In 1751 he published Amelia; in 1754 he resigned his judicial office and traveled to Lisbon, where his death occurred at the age of 47. He was one of the last of the great literary figures to combine a successful career in public service with an equally successful mission (in the light of later appreciation of his accomplishments) in literature.

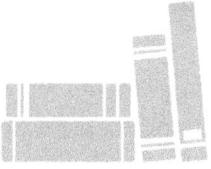

JOSEPH ANDREWS

BRIEF SUMMARY

BOOK I

Lady Booby, journeying with her husband to the social season in London from their estate in Somersetshire, is attended by her waiting-gentlewoman Mrs. Slipslop and her footman Joseph Andrews. Even before Sir Thomas' untimely death, Lady Booby showed many marks of favor to Joey, but after her husband's demise her importunings become more obvious. Angered by the chaste Joseph's refusals, she orders Slipslop to dismiss him (which she does, with misgivings, since she too had designs on him). On his way back to Lady Booby's country seat where he had been raised, Joseph is beaten, robbed, and stripped by highwaymen, then reluctantly rescued by the occupants of a coach, all of whom were utterly lacking in charitable affections except a young postilion, who gave Joseph his great coat. At the Dragon inn, only the chambermaid, Bett, takes an interest in nursing Joseph to health, the Tow-wouses (the owners) give him grudging accommodation, and a surgeon and parson (Barnabas) pay him only the most perfunctory attention. To his great surprise, Joseph encounters his old friend (and curate of Lady Booby's parish) Parson Abraham Adams at the inn, that gentleman being on his way to London to sell his sermons. Having been introduced to a bookseller by Barnabas, Adams tries to interest him in his sermons, but to no avail, the negotiations being broken off by an uproar created by Mr. Towwouse, who discovers her own chambermaid Betty in bed with her husband, whither Betty had repaired after having thrown herself at Joseph, and having been rejected by him.

BOOK II

Adams has actually forgotten his sermons, which causes him to accompany Joseph back to their parish. Using the system of "ride and tie," Adams set out on foot, leaving Joseph behind with the horse, which he shortly discovers he has to abandon, having no money to pay for his feed. Entering another inn, Adams listens to the conversation of two lawyers who respectively applaud and upbraid the morals and judgment of a local justice (the reason being, as the host explains, that they had argued a case before him). Mr. Slipslop, and then Joseph, happen along, Adams joining Slipslop and the other ladies in a coach, one of whom tells a lengthy story about Leonora and Bellarmine (a sentimental story of the type that the **realism** of *Joseph Andrews* is a reply to). At the next inn, Adams rebukes the surly host, who had made a disparaging comment about Joseph's injured leg, and found himself in a fist fight with the host, whose wife then hurled a pan full of hog's blood at him, while a certain Miss Graveairs and a much-travelled gentleman cluck disapprovingly, Joseph now entered the coach, leaving Adams to walk, and he meets a man who descants at length on the virtue of bravery, but runs away when he hears sounds of an attack. It is Fanny, Joseph's beloved, who is rescued from a would-be ravisher by Adams, the two of them, however, being arrested by mob of bird-batters through a wily tick on the part of Fanny's attacker.

Brought before an ignorant and inept justice, they are released only by the timely intervention of Squire Booby. At the next inn, Adams and Fanny encounter Joseph; there is a display of tender affection between the lovers, and of bad grace by Slipslop (who is chagrined to find Fanny, an obstacle to her designs on Joseph, and stalks off). Adams, impecunious as usual, tries to borrow money from Parson Trulliber, only to discover that he is a gross uncharitable hypocrite, but is then bailed out by a poor country peddler. Travelling on, they meet an apparently benevolent squire, who promises Adams a great deal and makes good on nothing, and they hear the story of the inn-keeper's life, who had himself been victimized by the same squire. The host is surprised to discover in Adams, however, not a sympathetic listener, but a stoic and ascete, who chides him for his interest in material things then walks out in high dudgeon.

BOOK III

Adams, Joseph, and Fanny, retreating from (as they imagine) a band of murderers, arrive at the cottage of Mr. Wilson, who gives them refreshment, and then entertains them with the story of his life-from the fleshpots of London to the retirement of a country farm with his wife (the former Harriet Hearty) - his only regret being the loss of a young son years before (Joseph, as it later develops). They travel on, Joseph and Adams disputing the effect which "public" schools have on national morality, and encounter a hare-hunt. The hunt master (a squire) sets his dogs on Adams; they are beaten off by him and Joseph, and the squire, feigning hospitality, invites them to his house, where he keeps a company of grotesque minions who give Adams a "roasting" until he finally understands the mockery they are making of him, gives the squire a dunking and leaves. They meet a priest at the next inn, who discourses to Adams on the contempt of wealth, and then reveals that he has no money for his bill, after which they retire for the night. In the morning, Fanny is abducted by the squire's henchmen, and Adams preaches stoic resignation to Joseph while both are tied to a bed-post. The timely arrival of Peter Pounce, Lady Booby's steward, and his attendants, brings about Fanny's rescue, but involves Adams in an argument with the unscrupulous and uncharitable Pounce, whose carriage Adams leaps from and continues the journey on foot.

BOOK IV

Lady Booby arrives at Booby Hall simultaneously with the other travellers, and proceeds to try to quash the intended marriage of Joseph and Fanny, first by threatening Adams with the loss of his living, if he should continue to publish the banns, and then by engaging the conniving Lawyer Scout to trump up a charge of theft against the lovers. Squire Booby (her nephew), happening to arrive with his wife Pamela, rescues them from the legal trap that Justice Frolick is about to snap, but tries to persuade Joseph against a marriage with one so far beneath him (Joseph, as everyone now thinks, being Pamela's brother). Lady Booby, not to be thwarted, next engages the services of Beau Didapper, who first by force and then by blandishments tries to seduce Fanny, but is beaten by Joseph. The lad is then admonished by Adams for repining at the trials Providence has set for him, but sees Adams suddenly brought to passionate outbursts by the (happily, false) news that his son has drowned. The arrival of the peddler (whose now deceased wife had formerly travelled with a gipsy band) brings the revelation that Joseph is not only the sister of Pamela, but also, of Fanny, which causes the lovers first to swoon and then to declare their intention of living together in Platonic friendship. This is quickly succeeded, however, by the arrival of Mrs. Andrews and Wilson, confirming the fact that Fanny is indeed an Andrews, but revealing that Joseph is the son of Wilson, and that they are free to marry after all. The wedding reception is held at Squire Booby's home, where he gives Fanny a gift of two thousand pounds, Adams a living of one hundred thirty pounds a year, and the peddler a position as exciseman. Lady Booby returns to London, where her next escapade obliterates Joseph's memory entirely.

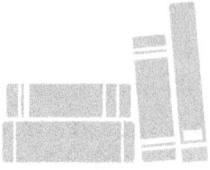

JOSEPH ANDREWS

TEXTUAL ANALYSIS

BOOK I

CHAPTER 1

In his fictional persona of an amiable earnest cicerone, anxious to ingratiate himself with his readers by relating a moral narrative, Fielding begins with what he pretends is a straightforward explanation of the tradition he is working in and the motives which have prompted him to write. He is going to write a "history" of good people, in the tradition of Plutarch and Nepos, and of such English biographies as those of Jack the Giant-killer, Guy of Warwick, and The Seven Champions of Christendom. But his special models, he declares, particularly valuable since they represent both the sexes, are the recent "histories' of the lives of Colley Cibber ("which deals in male virtue") and of Pamela Andrews.

Comment

The full range of Fielding's ironic tone is spread before us immediately. By defining the limits of his perceptive powers so narrowly (in lumping Jack the Giant-Killer together with Plutarch), and by archly confusing true history and biography with fiction and romance, Fielding establishes his straight-faced (and somewhat wooden-headed) fictional personality. He is thus able to pretend so effectively that he has really been favorably impressed by the recent autobiography of Colley Cibber, a smug defense of an often dilettantish, rakish, and time-serving career, and by Richardson's novel *Pamela: or Virtue Rewarded,* a sentimental piece of fiction extolling the chastity of Pamela Andrews, a heroine who does not appear, however, to have been above an artful manipulation of her attractiveness.

His own "authentic history," the narrator declares, is concerned with the manner in which Pamela's brother Joseph preserved his purity in the midst of great temptations.

CHAPTER 2

Since it is traditional for literary heroes to be provided with a lineage, Fielding humorously traces Joseph's ancestry, though he finds himself unable to go beyond his great-grandfather, an excellent cudgel-player in these parish. Thus forced to waive this requirement, the author takes refuge in the obvious fact that Joseph must have as many ancestors (though his family tree is obscure) as the best man living, but decides to offer the hypothesis that he has none-that he has, for argument's sake, sprung full-blown from a dunghill. Does this mean that his virtues may not be praised? Is it impossible for him to acquire honor? (Fielding is half-serious here, since the socially mobile mercantilist class, and a degenerating nobility are giving new point to the old medieval peasants' complaint: "When Adam delved and Eva span / Who was then the gentleman?") Fielding now describes Joseph's early life as an apprentice to a country lord, Sir Thomas Booby, an uncle of Mr. Booby (Fielding thus fills out the name of Pamela's would-be seducer, Mr. Booby). Beginning as a scarecrow, and advancing successively through the ranks of kennel-boy, stable-boy, and jockey, Joseph made a reputation for his strength and agility as well as for his good character, and found himself at the age of seventeen a footboy to the Lady Booby. Among his other graces, his psalm-singing brought him to the attention of the curate Mr. Abraham Adams (who will, of course, play a major role in the book).

CHAPTER 3

Parson Adams was a scholar, learned in the Greek and Latin tongues, to which he added great abilities in the modern languages, and some competence in the Oriental ones. He was extremely good-natured but very naive-generous but "simple" (in the sense of frank, candid). He had the handsome income (Fielding is sarcastic here) of 23 pounds a year, which allowed him, however, little show of opulence considering that he had a wife and six children.

Adams was marvelously impressed with Joseph's ability to answer a number of rather perfunctory bible-study questions, and upon inquiry learned that the lad had been put to school by his father at the expense of six-pence a week to learn to read and write, and that while in service all his leisure time had been spent reading the Bible, the *Whole Duty of Man* (a pious treatise), Thomas a Kempis (that is, the Imitation of Christ), and Baker's *Chronicle of the Kings of England.*

Comment

The reader is confronted at the outset by the problem of determining the author's attitude toward his chief characters, Joseph and Adams, and toward popular and conversational standards of goodness and morality. It is easy to imagine Fielding, a sophisticated man of belles-lettres and the London beau monde, sneering at the naivete of Adams and the simple-minded literary fare of Joseph. But the matter is by no means so easy to resolve. There is unquestionably something gauche about Adams, but he is good and high-minded; and while Joseph's range of interests is singularly narrow, one can hardly quarrel with his reading of the Bible and a Kempis. The faint shimmer of **irony** which plays about the heads of these characters, at least, never vitiates their essential wholesomeness.

Neither Sir Thomas nor Lady Booby had any understanding or appreciation of the parson's good parts, though he enjoyed the respect of Mrs. Slipslop, the waiting-gentlewoman, apparently because he gave her the occasion of disputing points of theology and thus displaying her mastery of "hard words." ("Hard words" is something of an eighteenth-century joke, since dictionaries of "hard words" were compiled specifically for women, about whose intellectual abilities there was still some good-humored speculation. Complicating the humor here is the fact that Mrs. Slipslop, like Congreve's Mrs. Malaprop, murders the language with impossible coinages and constructions.) Adams, taking advantage of his reputation with that lady, asked her to use her good offices to have the Boobys leave Joseph in his tutelage (mainly for Latin) when they should leave for London. Slipslop, however, refused. (There is only the slightest suggestion here that Lady Booby and Slipslop both have an interest in Joseph that is more than merely official.)

CHAPTER 4

After arriving in London, Joseph begins to feel the "corrupting" effect of city life. He affects the latest fashion in haircuts, and attends the opera, playhouses, and other assemblies. But his decline never goes beyond a mere superficial foppishness-his morals remain unimpaired.

Lady Booby rejoiced in the "life" she now detected in Joseph, and followed it up with familiarities, sly leers, and other "innocent freedoms" a lady of her station could carry off without criticism. Finally, however, Joseph and Lady Booby walking arm-in-arm one day, became the prey of Lady Tittle and Lady Tattle, who proceeded with dispatch to ruin their reputations, and might have succeeded if two fresh scandals had not ensued on the following day. No amount of slander, however, had the slightest impression on Joseph, nor could he be induced to relax his impeccable conduct towards his lady in the minutest detail.

CHAPTER 5

Without warning, Sir Thomas Booby died, and his "disconsolate" widow kept to her room for six days with no other company than Slipslop (and three female friends, to make up a card party). On the seventh day she summoned Joseph, and with hints, blandishments, and cajolings, as well as by hypothetical (though transparent) examples of ladies who might fall in love with him, and finally by the most obvious invitation for him to make the most of her undefended situation, she tempts him to lay aside his virtue. Embarrassed and stammering, the youth tries to discover a means by which he can retreat without humiliating his lady. Incensed at the rebuff, but pretending outrage at what she calls his hypocritical behavior, Lady Booby dismisses Joseph in a rage.

CHAPTER 6

The chapter begins with a letter written by Joseph to his sister Pamela, in which (in his very ingenuous fashion) he reveals (a) that there was no love lost between Sir Thomas and Lady Booby; (b) that he is of the strong opinion that Lady Booby had designs upon his person not unlike those amours he had observed in stage plays at Covent Garden; (c) his fear that he will be discharged, with his intention to leave London, a "bad place," and return to visit Parson Adams.

No sooner was the letter dispatched than Joseph encountered Mrs. Slipslop. (Fielding now describes her in detail.) She is an unmarried woman of about forty-five (all women were accorded the courtesy title of Mrs. in Fielding's day), who, after one slip in her youth, has remained a good maid ever since. The author presents with a great show of diffidence and delicacy the rude facts of her appearance; she is fat, gross, red pimply, bovine in her upper parts, and gimpy-legged. She has been trying to curry Joseph's favor for a long time, with all sorts of treats and allurements, but with no success. She justifies her amorous inclinations, by convincing herself that her long enforced abstinence has entitled her to a fling.

Continuing the narrative, the author relates that Mrs. Slipslop, taking advantage of Joseph's downcast condition, plied him with wine and oblique passionate entreaties. But the combination of her physical repulsiveness and her conversational obtuseness together with Joseph's stern morality, proves too strong a barrier.

Fielding closes the chapter with a mock Homeric **simile**, in which he compares the passion-stricken Mrs. Slipslop to a "hungry tigress," or a "voracious pike," ready to devour its prey, when suddenly the ringing of her lady's bell "delivered the intended martyr from her clutches."

SUMMARY (CHAPTERS 1-6)

The narrative so far has been a rather rambling affair, with a great deal of personal comment by Fielding in his role of amiable expositor. At best, we expect the plot to turn somehow on Joseph's adventures in "preserving his virtue," though it seems on the surface a slender thread on which to hang a novel of this length. The reader's main response so far is to the book as **parody, satire, irony,** and moral commentary.

1. **Parody**: It has, of course, always been recognized that *Joseph Andrews* is to some extent a **parody** of *Pamela*. So far, the following elements have been introduced:

    a. The irreproachable heroine (here, of course, "hero"), who is a non-pareil of chastity, and called "Joseph" after his chaste Biblical prototype.

    b. Two would-be seducers (who, in an amusing distortion of the facts of male and female psychology, are women rather than men).

    c. The epistolary method (Joseph's letter to Pamela).

    d. **Parody** of style - not particularly noteworthy yet, though there are in Joseph's letter traces of the astounding self-possession and unshakable aplomb of Richardson's heroine. There are also humorous parodies of "heroic style" in the tracing of lineage, and in the Homeric simile.

2. **Satire**: There are a number of open, sarcastic **allusions** to Colley Cibber's autobiography, in particular to the complacent and sanguine attitude taken toward the matter of human vices.

3. **Irony**: If irony may be taken broadly as the more or less clear indication of an author's awareness of discrepancies between appearance and reality-both in the nature of the universe and in the relationship between act and motive in the individual-it is apparent that Fielding is an ironist. Among many things, he calls attention to:

    a. The disparity between the relative influence of good people and of books about good people (because of their circulation).

    b. The human tendency to mask self-seeking motives in guises of public policy or other altruistic forms.

    c. The indistinguishable blending of genuine idealism with quixotic impracticality in the same individual.

4. **Moral commentary:** For all his obliqueness and sophisticated wit, we are never really in doubt about Fielding's scorn for the moral obtuseness of Sir Thomas and Lady Booby, for instance, and his sympathy for the open-heartedness of Parson Adams. This **theme** will expand as the book progresses into an impressively various catalogue of knaves and fools.

CHAPTER 7

Pretending a disinterested analysis of the varying effects love has on different human dispositions (the "cultivated" Lady Booby, and the "coarser" Mrs. Slipslop), the narrator actually presents the amusing confrontation between the mistress and the servant, in which it is to both their interests to preserve that relationship, even while they are in conflict over the fact that both have conceived a passion for the footman, Joseph. Imagining that she had successfully transmuted her love into disdain, Lady Booby summoned Slipslop and interrogated her about the young man. Dissembling, Slipslop alleged that she had not seen him that morning, and replied to her mistress's accusations that he was a wild fellow with an indictment of Joseph as one given to drinking, swearing, and wenching. The lady orders his dismissal, whereupon Slipslop, seeing she has gone too far, tries to defend him. They realize each other's vulnerability; and the matter is concluded with Lady Booby summoning Joseph once again. Fielding ends the chapter with a rhetorical apostrophe to Love, which has the power so to metamorphose human beings, playing havoc with their senses and their understanding.

> Comment

The apostrophe (one of numerous rhetorical figures employed with deliberate **irony** by Fielding) has the effect of lampooning the very notion of a woman's languishing for love. Typically, it is the man (in a long literary tradition going back to the medieval Romance of the Rose) who suffers impairment of his senses, physical pangs, and visionary delusions as a result of love-sickness-what was actually regarded as a disease, the "lover's malady of hereos," as it is termed by Chaucer.

CHAPTER 8

The narrator continues with a high rhetorical flourish (referring, in fact, in the chapter title, to his own "fine writing"), cloaking the fact of Joseph's attendance upon Lady Booby in **allusions** to mythology, and pretending to a high degree of fairness in his evaluation of this member of the fair sex-an impartiality which takes the form of grammatical backing and filling with all sorts of qualifying clauses and phrases, amounting to an excruciating degree of punctilio. (Actually, it is a scathing indictment of superannuated belles, who reform only when there is no longer any possibility of attempts upon their honor.)

In a lengthy paragraph, the author details Joseph's physical attractiveness, and his handsome features in a manner which would be appropriate for a woman, but hardly for a man, and then proceeds with his story. Lady Booby set forth the charge against the footman, namely, that he has gotten one of the serving-maids with child. (This, of course, only to give herself a hold over Joseph and bend him to her will.) He replied with expressions of amazement and assertions of innocence, admitting to nothing more than occasional offers of a kiss. Taking the opening, Lady Booby invited Joseph to kiss her, but was once more politely rebuffed, while Joseph maintained the hope that his virtue would never be overcome by base inclinations. To his mistress' astonished inquiry as to how a boy could thus talk of his virtue, the young man replied:

> Madam ... that boy is the brother of Pamela, and would be ashamed that the chastity of his family, which is preserved in her, should be stained in him. If there are such men as your ladyship mentions, I am sorry for it; and I wish they had an opportunity of reading over those letters, which my father hath sent me of my sister Pamela's; nor do I doubt but such an example would amend them.

Lady Booby's wrathful outburst, accusing Joseph of an insulting reference to her relative (Mr.B__), and pretending that her offer of favors was only meant to determine his guilt or innocence, was followed by her immediate dismissal of Joseph from her service. Joseph having left, she rang the bell violently, to which Slipslop responded almost at once, since she had been applying her ear to the keyhole during the preceding encounter.

CHAPTER 9

Being commanded by her mistress to arrange with the steward for Joseph's dismissal, Slipslop (now that she has something on Lady Booby) speaks up freely and pertly: "If you will turn away every footman ... that is a lover of the sport, you must soon open the coach door yourself." Chiding Slipslop for her impertinence,

Lady Booby nevertheless suspects that she is privy to her secret, and rather than run the risk of being exposed she decides to put up with the insult. Hence she called up the steward herself, and ordered him to turn Joseph out. Then, priming Slipslop with a small cordial, she began to reason with her, and found that it took effect. Slipslop, not so foolish as to give up a certain position, and seeing that her mistress' mind was made up with respect to Joseph, relented and was given some presents as a peace offering.

Lady Booby emerged from the affair not quite so equably. Not that she feared she had made her feelings too patent to Joseph, nor that Slipslop could not be managed with a small bribe, but that she did not, indeed, know whether in truth she had conquered her passion. In her mind her feelings took the form of a trial in which Love interceded for Joseph, Honor and Pity tried to vindicate him, and Pride and Revenge to indict him.

COMMENT

Fielding is of course using the allegorical scene here only partly in a facetious way. It is in a tradition (perhaps the dying gasp of a tradition) of rendering interior psychological states through the inter-actions of allegorized abstractions, particularly the medieval **theme** of the Four Daughters of God-a method of clarifying the notion of the human soul's final grace or damnation through a celestial trial scene in which Mary (Love) intercedes, Mercy and Peace (Honor and Pity) defend, and Truth and Justice (Pride and Revenge) prosecute the soul. Fielding complicates the **metaphor**, but brings it further in the direction of modern relevance, by alluding to Westminster trials he has seen, prosecuted by the typological figures of the lawyers Bramble and Puzzle.

In a self-conscious **allusion** to his tortured similes, Fielding closes the chapter.

CHAPTER 10

Finally perceiving that his mistress' dismissal of him was absolute, Joseph brooded over his misfortune in being handsome, and then sat down to open a letter to Pamela. "O Pamela!" he declares, "my mistress is fallen in love with me - that is, what great folks call falling in love, - she has a mind to ruin me."

Comment

The humor and the **irony** in Joseph's use of the word "ruin" at this point almost defies definition. At some point, apparently in the late seventeenth century, it took on the meaning "to bring dishonor to a woman," but suffered constantly from the ambiguity of the fact that moral "ruination" was frequently accompanied by financial success. Defoe's *Moll Flanders* (and he uses the word constantly) is just a "ruined maid," - one who has cannily manipulated her sexual commodities into economic affluence. Richardson, too, was aware of the ambiguity, for in Pamela we find the following conversation: [Pamela] "I dare say, you think yourself, that he intends my ruin." "I hate," said she [Mrs. Jewkes-the servant conniving at Pamela's seduction] "that foolish word, your ruin!-Why, ne'er a lady in the land may live happier than you if you will, or be more honourably used." "Well, Mrs. Jewkes," said I, "I shall not, at this time, dispute with you about the words ruin and honourable: for I find we have quite different notions of both." The ultimate step in the word's history is probably the poem by Thomas Hardy, "The Ruined Maid," which begins as follows:

"O, 'Melia, my dear, this does everything crown!

Who would have supposed I should meet you in Town?

And whence such fair garments, such prosperity?"

"O didn't you know I'd been ruined?" said she.

It was certainly obvious to Fielding that "ruination" in this sense is hardly in the offing for Joseph.

Praising Parson Adams for his wholesome advice and example, and Pamela for her encouraging letters, he asks her to pray for the preservation of his chastity. Joseph then proceeds to pick up his wages from the steward Peter Pounce (who, it develops, has been collecting fifty percent interest on advance wages). Taking the pittance which remains to him, Joseph strips off his livery, borrows a frock from one of the servants, and sets off for the country.

SUMMARY (CHAPTERS 7-10)

We note in these chapters a closer attention to character analysis, greater virtuosity with stylistic tricks, and an increasing tendency to identify specific social evils:

1. Character:

    a. The relationship between Lady Booby and Slipslop-their verbal fencing with one another and growth in understanding of their mutual dependence-is developed at great length.

b. While we hardly achieve any sympathy for Lady Booby, we do, despite Fielding's sardonic portrait, come to a greater appreciation of what it means to be jaded toast, and to have to fear a system which puts even those whose vices are private at the mercy of gossiping servants.

c. Similarly, Slipslop hardly engenders a feeling of pathos in the reader, but he comes to recognize the futility of a servant's aspiring to any independence of situation in such a rigidly structured social world.

2. Style:

   a. Fielding employs standard rhetorical figures in an obvious and exaggerated way both to ridicule affection and to qualify potentially serious meanings which might be imputed to him. Thus the apostrophe to Love and the allegorical trial of Joseph in Lady Booby's psyche produce laughter at her expense at the same time that they reclaim Fielding from any possible excess of solemnity.

   b. The lofty rhetoric of the opening of Chapter 8 combines **parody** of Richardson's sentimental loquaciousness with sarcastic criticism (by the very fact of vagueness and abstractness) of feminine libido and eleventh-hour reforms.

3. In addition to his general attack on the vanity of the beaumonde in the persons of the Boobys, Fielding presents, among other topical allusions:

    a. a picture of avarice, in the gouging steward Peter Pounce.

    b. a preliminary portrait (in the **episode** of Bramble and Puzzle) of the confused state of the law, and the difficulty of obtaining justice.

CHAPTER 11

The previous chapter having completed the narrative of Joseph's employment by Lady Booby, and his journey now about to begin, Fielding once more rambles on genially about certain matters which he feels the reader ought to be made acquainted with. (Pretending, in fact, that his book is absolutely planless, the author remarks disarmingly that "he is a sagacious reader who can see two chapters before him.")

Joseph's extraordinary haste, he explains, is by no means due to his desire to see his parents or even his sister Pamela but to visit once again a young girl, poor but beautiful, with whom he had been long acquainted and for whom he had a most tender affection. Only Adams' counsels of thrift and foresight had prevented their marrying before this. Their previous parting was indeed a scene of profound pathos.

Comment

At this point Fielding archly remarks that the separation of Joseph from Fanny (for such was her most unromantic name) was made even more painful by the fact that she could neither read nor write, the incessant exchange of letter of Richardson's type of epistolary novel thus being made impossible for them.

Setting forth on his way, Joseph encounters a hailstorm and is forced to take refuge in an inn, where he is joined by another servant of his acquaintance, who happens to be riding and leading an extra horse of his master's. After draining a pot of ale together, they set off on horseback.

CHAPTER 12

At two in the morning, his friend being forced to turn off, Joseph proceeded on foot, but had not gone far before he was waylaid by ruffians, robbed of his money, and stripped of all his clothing. He lay a long hour in a ditch until stagecoach happened along the postilion, attracted by his groans, halted the team. He was berated for this by the coachman, and rebuked by several of the passengers: a lady, who was horrified at the thought of a naked man being taken aboard; a gentleman, who feared that they too might be robbed if they did not make haste; and a lawyer, who wished that they might have passed by without notice, but who was now concerned that they might all be brought before the bar as accomplices if they failed to take him up. The coachman stood pat on the matter of Joseph's fare, until he was bullied into submission by the lawyer. Joseph himself, however, not insensible to all these objections, refused to enter the coach (though he was bleeding and shivering with cold) until he should be provided with suitable covering. None but the position (who of course could least afford it) could be persuaded to part with an overcoat. Wearing the postilion's coat. Joseph was lifted into the coach.

A short distance further on the coach was itself waylaid by the same ruffians, who took from the lady a bottle of brandy (though she swore the bottle contained only perfume), and from the others all the money they had about them. When they had safely departed, the lawyer produced a pair of pistols which he said he would have used, if only he had been able to get at them, and the gentleman began to grow extremely facetious at Joseph's expense, making a number of obscene jokes and puns concerning his nakedness and the proximity of the lady.

Comment

Fielding's own sophisticated tone has the tendency to soften momentarily the vicious (and rather obvious) attack on the greedy, self-seeking, absolutely un-Christian members of the London upper crust. "Charity" resides only in the poor postilion, who, as Fielding notes, was later transported for robbing a hen-roost. Joseph meets a similar reception at the next inn. It is the serving-maid who warns him, feeds him, and runs for a doctor. The host (Mr. Tow-wouse) merely tolerates his presence, for which he is in fact loudly chided by his wife, who carries on a long tirade about the way in which he is impoverishing their house by taking in impecunious vagabonds. When the henpecked Mr. Tow-wouse pleads the excuse of "common charity" his wife reject him with a vulgar expletive and complains that they are being "ruin'd by your charity."

Comment

We may note here not only the common obsession so many characters have about being "ruined," but also the important ambiguity which surrounds the word "charity." It is, in fact, probably in the eighteenth century that the change from the original meaning of "love" (the caritas of St. Paul's "the greatest of these is charity") to the meaning of institutionalized doles for the indigent" takes place most rapidly. Without too much explicit moralizing Fielding is able to satirize the appalling selfishness of a number of social types.

To the surgeon's news that Joseph will probably lose his life, Mr. Tow-wouse screams about the expense of a funeral, and stalks out in search of Betty (the maid) to upbraid her.

CHAPTER 13

The surgeon who had examined Joseph warned him that he was in great danger and that "if the malign concoction of his humours should cause a suscitation of his fever, he might soon grow delirious, and incapable to make his will."

Comment

At one stroke Fielding encompasses the two chief complaints leveled against doctors by satirists for ages-their venality and their tendency to use medical jargon to impress patients with their skill and importance. It is not that this surgeon is greedy, but that his chief concern is with Joseph's last testament.

In this dread case the local parson (Mr. Barnabas) was sent for, and arrived at Joseph's room only to overhear the patient uttering a mournful soliloquy. (It is actually a high rhetorical outburst on the **theme** of the superiority of virtue to worldly pleasure, and of resignation to the Divine Will.) Barnabas retreated down the stairs claiming that he found the patient very light-headed, and uttering nothing but a "rhapsody of nonsense."

> Comment

Except for the inflated rhetoric, Joseph's speech, while extremely ingenuous, makes excellent sense especially from a clerical point of view. It is a criticism of Barnabas' own worldliness that he finds no sense in it.

Later, when Barnabas managed to engage the patient in conversation, Joseph uttered an understandable sentiment of regret at dying and leaving behind a young woman of the character of Fanny, and the parson once more demonstrates his very perfunctory grasp of a real piety by admonishing the lad that he was guilty of a "criminal despondence" by refusing to accept his death more hospitably. More conversation between them only serves to reveal Joseph's humanity and the hypocritical posturing of the parson.

CHAPTER 14

A grave stranger entered the inn at dusk, and took his place with the others at the fireplace, the conversation turning on the recent robbery. Mrs. Tow-wouse carried on with her complaints and Betty with her defense of Joseph, while the stranger contemplated the "sweetness" of the hostess's nature, which (he thought) was expressed in her face better than Hogarth himself might have done. (Hogarth, of course, is the famous illustrator of London low life, in such works as *The Rake's Progress*.) Fielding provides a detailed description of her face, with such details as a "forehead [which] projected in the middle, and thence descended in a declivity to the top of the nose." Without even any acquaintance with the injured guest, the stranger was able to conceive a great compassion for him. (As we later learn, the stranger is Parson Adams and knows Joseph very well indeed.)

The doctor, with an air of extraordinary self-importance, began to issue pronouncements on the patient's condition, with impressive references to Galen and Hippocrates, and received only slight demurrals from the stranger whom he proceeded to rebuke with pedantic **allusions** to Latin and Greek medical authors.

Comment

The stranger (Adams) has espoused the cause of empirical medical practice against the doctor, who follows the classical authorities, so that the argument takes the form of experience vs. authority, an old issue in medicine. Satirists for centuries had attacked extreme forms of both positions, Moliere's Diafoirus (in *Le Malade Imaginaire*) being an outstanding instance of medical book learning, and Jonson's "Doctor Empiric" in one of his epigrams) an example of the trial-and-error school:

When men of old a dangerous disease did 'scape

They gave a cock to Aesculape.

Let me give two, who doubly am set free,

From my disease's danger - and from thee.

The doctor's jargon-ridden recital was interrupted by cries from without, where some men arrived with one of the thieves who had been captured, along with part of the loot. The stranger recognized Joseph's cloak, and bounded up the stairs where he found the youth in bed. As they conversed, the mob below engaged in a dispute over the right to the disposition of the clothes, and the reward for the capture. The chapter ends with the thief protesting his innocence amid the wrangling of all the Philadelphia lawyers seated around the fire.

CHAPTER 15

When events seemed to indicate that Joseph might be no vagabond but a gentleman indeed, Mrs. Tow-wouse abated her malice somewhat. Even Barnabas and the surgeon paid the youth a visit when it was learned that he had a piece of gold in his possession, but Adams assumed the role of his staunch defender.

Left alone with Joseph, Adams revealed the purpose of his London visit, which was to arrange for the publication of three volumes of sermons of his own composition, since he was in need of additional income. Even so, Joseph was welcome to use any or all of the small amount of money he had with him. At Adams' insistence that he would soon be well, the lad managed to eat a light meal, amidst the renewed concern of Mrs. Tow-wouse, Barnabas, and the doctor, all of whom imagined that they might profit from his acquaintance. In the absence of a parish lawyer, indeed, the parson and the doctor vied with each other in a display of legal knowledge centering around the conviction of the accused thief.

In another declamatory passage in the high style, the author apostrophizes Vanity (because of the vanity the two men display in their legal wrangling):

> . . . how little is thy force acknowledged, or thy operations discerned! How wantonly dost thou deceive mankind under different disguises! Sometimes thou dost wear the face of pity, sometimes of generosity: nay

thou hast the assurance even to put on those glorious ornaments which belong only to heroic virtue. Thou odious, deformed monster! whom priests have railed at, philosophers despised, and poets ridiculed; is there a wretch so abandoned as to own thee for an acquaintance in public? - yet how few will refuse to enjoy thee in private? nay thou art the pursuit of most men through their lives . . .

Comment

The mocking air of scientific analysis (the opposition, for example, force and operation), the elaborate attention to balance and antithesis in sentence structure, the echoes of biblical style in the familiar pronouns and **cliches** like "glorious ornaments," all tend to subvert the apparently serious moralistic **theme** of the passage. The seriousness is undercut even further by Fielding's admission at the end that "I have introduced thee for no other purpose than to lengthen out a short chapter."

SUMMARY (CHAPTERS 11-16)

These chapters cover Joseph's adventures on the high road leading away from London-the robbery and beating, the stage-coach ride, and the reception at the inn (at the Sign of the Dragon) presided over by the Tow-wouses. Coherence thus far seems to depend very little on intricate plotting, more on the inherent probability and credibility of the events which befall the youth-events likely enough to occur on the open road and in the inns of eighteenth century England. The substance of this section lies in the presentation of a number of character types, the deepening of the **theme** of the viciousness of affectation and self-aggrandizement, and the initial presentation of the character of Parson Adams.

1. Character:

    a. We meet several of the age-old targets of **satire**: the pompous, theory-spouting doctor; the crafty, venal lawyer; the hypocritical cleric (Barnabas). Several other perennial human delinquents are also paraded before us: the modish lady (in the coach); the uxorious husband (Tow-wouse); the wife who is a shrew and harridan (Mrs. Tow-wouse); and a number of minor figures connected with the robbery incident, all of whom are avaricious and hypocritical.

    b. "Good Characters": clearly, in addition to Adams, the postilion who parts with his coat, and Betty, the tender-hearted maid.

2. **Theme**: Fielding's theme begins to appear in the opposition between characters whose hypocrisy, vanity, and avarice lead them to a course of legalistic self-seeking and characters whose basically good intentions reveal an expansive sort of Christian charity. This **theme** will of course undergo modification later, when deception and self-deception are seen to afflict even fundamentally good persons.

3. Introduction of Adams: When Adams first appears he is referred to (in a generally approving portrait) as a "grave stranger." "Gravity," indeed, will be Adams'

central problem; when it turns to over-solemnity, as in the unrealistic attempt to peddle his sermons, it can make him ridiculous; yet, when he loses it entirely, and gambols about the room snapping his fingers, he is also ridiculous. The proper degree of gravity, without affectation, may be said to be one of the ideals toward which his experiences move him.

CHAPTER 16

In roundabout and facetious (though typically amusing) fashion, the author describes the escape of the thief; he "had modestly withdrawn himself by night, declining all ostentation" etc. The hopes of all involved of some part in a reward suddenly turn to fears of being accused of negligence or complicity, but Barnabas declares that since the escape was by night there could be no indictment.

Adams, deciding to return home with Joseph, then tries to borrow enough money from Tow-wouse, optimistically offering his nine volumes of manuscript sermons as collateral. Tow-wouse of course remained evasive. After a short time Adams found himself in conversation with Barnabas, a long mutual lament over the unpopularity of morality, the hardships suffered by the clergy, and the difficulty of printing one's sermons.

With nothing resolved, Adams again visited Joseph, finding him well determined on the day of their departure. The chapter ends with the delivery of a message informing Adams that Barnabas had some business with him.

CHAPTER 17

Barnabas' business was to introduce Adams to a bookseller who had chanced to pay him a visit. Overjoyed, Adams took two or three turns about the room "in an ecstasy," snapping his fingers.

Comment

This characteristic of Adams is the external symbol of the element of naivete and gaucheness in Adams' personality. It is by no means a damning trait, but it suggests a kind of saintly inability to come to terms with the workaday world. No reader expects for a moment that the bookseller is going to offer Adams a contract at all, let alone leap at the chance of publishing his sermons.

Absolutely untutored in the way of driving a bargain, Adams expressed his great delight at the meeting, informing the bookseller of his own very good fortune as well. The bookseller promised merely to take the manuscript along and send him an opinion, whereupon the conversation comes around to a comparison between sermons and plays (plays obviously being far more marketable than sermons), a comparison Adams objects to. "But is there no difference between conveying good or ill instructions to mankind?" said Adams: "Would not an honest mind rather lose money by the one, than gain it by the other?" he declares with a degree of philosophical abstraction rivaling Plato's, to which (with fine existential common sense) the bookseller retorts that he is no enemy to sermons except for the fact that they do not sell.

(There follows a long discussion between the two men, in which Adams reveals his attitudes as they appear in the sermons. They are of course idealistic in the extreme, and every syllable he utters in defense of his opinions only convinces the bookseller of their unsuitability.) They are interrupted by an uproar upstairs. Mrs. Tow-wouse, having apprehended her husband in bed with Betty, was screaming indignant complaints at Tow-wouse and obscene imprecations at the unfortunate maid. Betty's limit is reached, however, when the hostess calls her a "b___," and with injured feelings she protests vehemently at being called a "she dog." All retire in confusion.

CHAPTER 18

This chapter begins with a "history of Betty," and expatiates on her warm-heartedness, which might have been successfully controlled in a nunnery but could hardly endure the "ticklish situation of a chambermaid at an inn." There is some facetious word-play by Fielding, on the ability of a certain young ensign to "raise a flame in her" (a punning reference to venereal disease), and how, while she "burnt for him, several others burnt for her." Though she then vowed perpetual chastity, "the rhetoric of John the hostler, with a new straw hat, and a pint of wine, made a second conquest over her."

Comment

The use of the language of the sentimental aristocratic romances here is in a long tradition of literary **burlesque** going back to such medieval examples as *The Tournament of Tottenham*, a poem which uses the **imagery** and vocabulary of alliterative chivalric romance to describe the contest to village lads mounted on plow-horses for the hand of the miller's daughter.

The history of Betty is preparation for the next **episode**. Betty had conceived a grand passion for Joseph, and one evening threw herself at him, modesty and reason together having been overcome. Only through force could the youth fend her off, a rejection which caused her to think of suicide, but only temporarily, since, passing Mr. Tow-wouse's chamber, she fell willing prey to his importunities. (This is the scene which Mrs. Tow-wouse stumbled upon.) The upshot of the entire matter was that Betty was discharged, and that Tow-wouse remained effectively in his wife's control for the rest of his days.

SUMMARY (CHAPTERS 16-18)

Fielding rounds off his first book, rather artificially, with two significant and parallel incidents: in one, Adams encounters the world of practical affairs in the form of a bookseller and comes off with his ideals unimpaired but with some scars in his sanguine temperament; in the other, Joseph encounters an attack on his chastity which he successfully surmounts. Despite the necessity (for purposes of **parody**) of making such characters as Betty and the Tow-wouses somewhat grotesque, the author never goes beyond what, in the last analysis, is credible. As for the plot, however, it is apparent from the adventitious manner in which events occur in those chapters that a reader who expects neatly woven plotting will be disappointed. The necessities of characterization and **theme**, rather than the logic of events, determine the inclusion of incident.

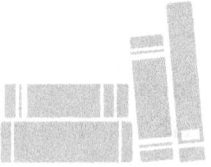

JOSEPH ANDREWS

TEXTUAL ANALYSIS

BOOK II

CHAPTER 1

As a way of beginning the second book, and of accounting for the fact that a work is divided into books and chapters, Fielding, with mock modesty, refers to literary authorship as a "trade," comparable to that of tailoring, with books and chapters answering to the tailor's stays and buckram. Or, to use the analogy of a long journey, the chapters may be regarded as inns, and the white pages between books as resting stages, wherein the traveller may reflect easefully on the regions he has passed through. (The chapter titles are the inscriptions over the gates.) And he claims sanction for the practice of division in the example of Homer (whose twenty-four books were perhaps intended as a compliment to the letters of the alphabet, to which he had "very particular obligations"), of Virgil, and of Milton. As a final facetious analogy, he adduces that of the butcher, who joints his meat as an assistance to the carver.

CHAPTER 2

Adams and Joseph were about to depart in opposite directions (since the parson still had his sermons to sell), when it was discovered that his saddle bag contained no sermons at all but a parcel of extra clothing. This accident making it necessary for Adams to return with Joseph, the bill was called for and paid by the parson with a guinea he had borrowed from a passing servant who had once been one of his parishioners. With only one horse between them, they decided to "ride and tie" (one rides ahead and leaves the horse for his companion who has set out on foot behind him). Adams set forth, while Joseph waited at the inn with the horse. The youth found himself in a dilemma, however, since he was unexpectedly presented with a bill for the horse's feed by the Tow-wouses, and had not the wherewithal to pay it. Since nothing could induce him to part with the gold piece which his beloved Fanny had given him, he was forced to leave on foot also.

Adams meanwhile was perfectly at ease, occupied in contemplating a passage in *Aeschylus* for the extent of three miles, without a thought for his companion.

Comment

Adam's propensity for quoting, musing about and arguing about obscure passages in ancient Greek authors is another aspect of his unworldliness and impracticality. It is hardly a vice, but while it is certainly innocuous to others, it is the source of some of the parson's own difficulties.

Coming upon a large pool in the road, Adams waded through it, wetting his clothes and shoes thoroughly, then discovering that if only he had looked over the hedge he would have seen a footpath around it. (This is yet another indication of the total impracticality of the parson-he can dispute the finest points of Greek grammar but cannot keep his shoes from getting soaked.) Finally growing fearful at Joseph's failure to arrive, and seeing no inn where he might dry his clothing, Adams sat down on a stile and pulled out his copy of *Aeschylus*; a passerby then directed him to a nearby inn.

CHAPTER 3

As the parson was seated in the inn, two horsemen rode up and entered. Their conversation-about a "comical adventure" involving a man who could not pay for his horse's hay-reminded Adams that this must indeed have been his own horse they were speaking of. Since the weather was vile, however, he could not leave to return to Joseph, and the three men sat down together over a mug of beer. To make conversation the parson inquired about a certain house he had passed earlier, and was treated to a violent difference of opinion concerning the character of the owner. One of the men was most reproachful, calling the owner a tyrant, a cruel master and a biased judge; the other in his turn praised the owner as being just the opposite-a fair landowner, the finest of masters, and the best justice of the peace in the kingdom. Upon their departure Adams, in astonishment, inquired of the innkeeper if it were possible that these two travellers were speaking of the same man. The host's opinion was that the owner was of neither extreme, not excessively liberal and yet no tyrant, not the worst master in the world but certainly none of the best; as for his qualities as a justice, the only case he had heard in recent years was one involving the very two men who had just left the inn. The host was certain that Adams would have no difficulty recognizing how the case had been decided. To Adam's shocked response to the lies they had told, the innkeeper calmly asked whether Adams himself had never told a lie. Out of love to one's self, he opined, lies were sometimes necessary. Out of love to yourself, replied Adams, you should always tell the truth.

Comment

Fielding uses this incident to dramatize the conflict between a purely ideal order of existence and a purely material one. "Self-love," as the host conceives of it, is the cupiditas (opposed to caritas) which St. Augustine considers the essential characteristic of the City of Man. "Self-love," as Adams regards it, is that respect for one's status as an intelligent, spiritual being, which the ancient philosophers thought of as the ultimate criterion for a man's actions. It is also the Pauline concept of self-love. A man who loves himself will not allow the "war in the members" to bring him to his own destruction. Of course, Adams' position is theoretically the "right" one, but he is asking a great deal of human nature.

At this point a coach drew up, from which emerged Mrs. Slipslop (who had previously extricated Joseph from his dilemma with the horse). She and Adams exchanged hearty greetings, and in a short time Joseph himself appeared. With Adams in the coach, and Joseph on horseback, the party proceeded, while Slipslop began to inform the parson of the state of affairs in the Booby household, praising her master and blaming her mistress (to the surprise of Adams, who had been accustomed to hearing her do just the reverse). Then, as they drew even with a great house standing some distance off, a lady in the coach identified it as the house of "the unfortunate Leonora, if one may justly call a woman unfortunate whom we must own at the same time guilty, and the author of her own calamity," and proceeded to the delight of all to tell her story.

CHAPTER 4

(This chapter, which is given the title "The History of Leonora, or the "Unfortunate Jilt," will be summarized very briefly since it has little to do with the main narrative line.)

Comment

Fielding apparently includes this story as an illustration of the extent to which refinement of manners ("good breeding") is able to camouflage the most sordid intrigues and emotional trifling. It also allows for intermittent reactions by Adams, Slipslop, and the other ladies in the coach, filling out their characterizations. Furthermore, the story is carried on partly through an exchange of letters in the excessively refined style characteristic of Richardson's Letter Writer (a handbook of model letters, mainly intended for the rising bourgeoisie who needed lessons in acceptable behavior).

Leonora, a gay and beautiful young woman, always the belle of the ball, consented after long entreaties to have Horatio, a young barrister, sue for her hand. After some initial coquettish maneuvers they come to an understanding about eventual marriage, an understanding, however, which is masked in the silly cultivated rhetoric of the letter-writing manuals. (Leonora, for instance, instead of "wedding day" speaks of "that blest day, when I shall experience the falsehood of a common assertion, that the greatest human happiness consists in hope.") During Horatio's protracted absence, Leonora's wandering eye was caught by a foppish gentleman named Bellarmine (a typical affecter of French fashions), and with the stimulus of the rich life which she felt sure would be hers, she transferred her affections to him. (In the evaluation of the lady-narrator, "what modesty had employed a full year in raising, impudence demolished in twenty-four hours.") With the encouragement of her aunt, Bellarmine determined to propose the match to Leonora's father, at which juncture Horatio returned to find the two together, and (with a good deal of empty bravado on both sides) a duel was arranged, and Bellarmine received, as it was thought, a mortal wound. At the news, Leonora beat her breast and tore her hair in anguish, wondering how she might regain the affections of Horatio, when she received a letter from Bellarmine declaring that the wound was slight, whereupon she paid him a visit to insure that she should not lose him. (The company now arrives at another inn, and the narrative is broken off.)

CHAPTER 5

The horse which Joseph was riding (Adams had borrowed it from his clerk) had the habit of falling on his knees at unexpected intervals, and had just pinned the youth's leg under him. The innkeeper's wife, a compassionate soul, was applying an ointment to Joseph's injury, when her husband, a surly fellow, began to berate her, and expressed a wish that if the leg were really bad it might be amputated forthwith. Adams chided the host for his inhumanity, and, receiving a scornful reply and an offer of violence, dealt him a blow on the nose. The host then answered with a blow but received a stroke from Adams which laid him flat. The host's wife, loyally coming to the assistance of her churlish mate, threw a pitcher of hog's blood at the parson's face, which made him a horrible spectacle to behold. Just at that moment Mrs. Slipslop ventured upon the scene and taking all in at a glance set upon the unfortunate woman and deprived her of handfuls of hair while she also rained blows at her face.

The uproar and the outcries of "Murder!" brought to the room the two gentlemen who had conversed with Adams at Tow-wouse's inn, a gentleman who had just returned from an Italian trip, and the several ladies who had been riding in the coach. The Italian traveller, addressing himself to Miss Graveairs (the haughty woman), reassured her by stating that there had only been a little boxing taking place, "which . . . to their disgracia the English were accustomata to," and went on with further remarks in an English spiced with Italian terms (and an egregious misquotation of Shakespeare), concluding that he had never "seen such a spectaculo" before.

Comment

A trip to Italy was de rigueur as part of the education of every well-to do young Englishman; Milton's famous Italian journey is a case in point. But there were, of course, many affected and dilettantish travellers as well (as indeed there are today, and in any age). The character is so universal, and so easily lampooned that it had become a stock figure in English comedy as early as Jonson's time. Sir Politic Would-be, in *Volpone*, is a character partly of this sort. Bellarmine, in his affection for things French, bears some analogy to the Italian traveller. What is being satirized (and what makes Fielding's art in this instance so timeless) is a human tendency to put oneself above one's fellow citizens by an involvement with things exotic and out-of-the-way. In extreme form the affectation is ludicrous.

The other two gentlemen immediately displayed their litigious natures by taking sides, the one advising the host and the other Adams of the damages they were certain to obtain by seeking legal redress.

Their re-entrance into the coach was retarded by Miss Graveairs' refusal to admit the injured Joseph as a passenger, despite the intercession of Adams and all the other passengers in his behalf, a fact which led to a quarrel between that lady and Mrs. Slipslop about people who give themselves airs (funny partly because Slipslop, even though she is a servant, takes on airs vicariously, as it were, because of the rank of Lady Booby). The matter was settled, however, by the opportune arrival of Miss Graveairs' father, who took her off in his down coach. Immediately, the other ladies began to dissect her character, while Slipslop declared herself astonished that she had refused to admit such a handsome young fellow (he was, after all, not a "wretched, miserable old object," that turns one's stomach), both of which facts qualify the apparent charity they had shown in standing up for Joseph's admission.

CHAPTER 6

(The lady continues her story of Leonora.) Leonora, once she had thrown custom and modesty aside, gave her passion unbridled indulgence, and began to reside almost constantly at Bellarmine's apartment. One result of this was a poison pen letter to Leonora's father, written by a woman out of a sense of "duty," acquainting him with the baseness of the role she was playing. Her father, however, paid not the slightest attention to it, being far more concerned with heaping up a fortune than with raising his children, whom he regarded as "an unhappy consequence of youthful pleasures." The father's greed, in fact, was largely to blame for the unfortunate fate which was Leonora's, for when Bellarmine came to ask for her hand and inquire about her dowry, he was told that there was not a penny to be had. Long arguments and persuasions were of no avail, and Bellarmine finally was compelled to leave. He sent an extraordinarily polite explanation to Leonora, filled with the most affecting compliments in French, and hoped that he might see her again in Paris if her father should ever oblige her to a match. Leonora was ever after disconsolate; Horatio remained unmarried, never uttering one word of reproach against Leonora's use of him, and managed to raise a considerable fortune. The lady's final evaluation of the affair is that Leonora probably "deserves pity for her misfortunes, sore than our censure for a behaviour to which the artifices of her aunt very probably contributed."

Comment

As an indication of changing sentiment, it is perhaps worth quoting a popular song of our own "gay nineties":

> She is more to be pitied than censured,
>
> She is more to be helped than despised;
>
> She is only a lassie who ventured
>
> Onto life's stormy path ill-advised.

Actually, the effect and the point of the entire Leonora story is to be seen in two things:

   a. in the disparity between the superficial, public expression of motive and sentiment by the characters themselves (partly accepted by the teller and the listeners, including Adams) and the actual motives of greed, desire for place, physical passion and so forth, which clearly underlie conduct no matter how the characters may dissemble.

b. in the various points of analogy between the world of the Leonora story and the world of country inns and high roads, which is the world of Adams and Joseph. Though they take on superficial differences the same basic qualities of hypocrisy, vanity, avarice, and so forth account for the personal drives of characters in all walks of life.

SUMMARY (CHAPTERS 1-6)

In these chapters Adams, rather than Joseph, occupies the center of the stage, as we see him in a series of adventures and confrontations designed to illustrate his saintly ineptitude for the hard give-and-take of daily living. There is one thing, however, at which he is not inept, and that is at dealing a hard blow-a characteristic which is in some ways the most ludicrous of all, considering his calling as a country parson. Additional points:

1. The author keeps alive his established fictional persona in such matters as:

    a. the facetious explanation of the reasons for chapter divisions, and

    b. stylistic archness, as when, describing the fight between Adams and the host, he declares that "Adams dealt him . . . a compliment over his face with his fist . . . [and] the host . . . returned the favor."

2. Some continued themes:

   a. The prevalence of a narrow legalistic view of human relations (the "two anonymous gentlemen" **episode**);

   b. The paucity of true Christian charity, and the corresponding emphasis on the rights of social position (Miss Graveairs' refusal to admit Joseph to the coach);

   c. Affectation as a hindrance to meaningful involvements between persons (the Italian traveller incident).

3. Characterization:

There is a good deal of repetition among Fielding's characters. Miss Graveairs, for instance, is not noticeably different from that earlier lady who refused to admit Joseph to the coach after he had been beaten, nor are the two legalistically minded travellers vastly different from the lawyer of that same earlier **episode**. For the most part, Fielding's characters are types and the types are not overnumerous; what the introduction of new characters serves to do is to impart a sense of a teeming, vital world in the inns and on the roads of England. And far more important than character or incident in themselves is the opportunity they provide Fielding for **parody**, **irony**, and generally facetious wit. Adams, of course, is the most fully drawn character and yet even he, thus far, can be reduced to a few idiosyncrasies-the passion for *Aeschylus*, the snapping of the fingers, the constant indigence, the clenched fist.

4. Structure:

The "story within a story" **episode** of "The Unfortunate Jilt" demands that the reader look for Fielding's meaning as it grows out of parallels and contrasts between widely separated characters and incidents. The rigidly defined social castes (breaking down, of course, in the eighteenth century) make it possible for the author to develop his conception of various subjects and motifs by showing them in operation among different classes of people. For example:

    a. Romantic love-the nature of this phenomenon is clarified by representing its effect on such diverse couples as Lady Booby and Joseph, Betty and John the hostler, Joseph and Fanny, and Leonora and Bellarmine.

    b. Protection of achieved position-Miss Graveairs' fear of riding in the same coach with a footman; Slipslop's pride over serving in a household where she herself has the charge of a number of minor servants; Joseph's admonition to the surly host to watch his language towards his "betters" (Adams).

CHAPTER 7

The story being finished, the travellers all noticed that Adams was walking ahead of the coach, having forgotten his horse back at the inn. As they tried to overtake him, he ran ahead impishly until he had put three miles between them, finally losing his way, however. He decided to read his *Aeschylus* until the coach should come up, but was disturbed by the sound of a gun, discharged by a man shooting partridge. They fell into conversation, which soon turned to the soldiers quartered in the neighborhood, a subject which elicited from the stranger cries of contempt for the cowardice of soldiers, and a passionate declaration that "a man who won't sacrifice his life for his country, deserves to be hanged, damn me."

Comment

Fielding's training in the character typology of theater comedy is perhaps responsible for this creation, for he is clearly the stock figure of the "braggart soldier" (like Jonson's Bobadill and Shakespeare's Falstaff), who, when the chips are down, turns tail and runs.

Adams remarked that he approved of his virtue but deplored his swearing, and then declaring that he would be delighted to commune with him, began upon an autobiographical discourse (what Fielding refers to as "the most curious [discourse] in this [and] perhaps in any other book").

CHAPTER 8

(The chapter title describes this as a "dissertation" in which Adams "appears in a political light." Adams is of course the most unpolitical of beings, and the discourse is little more than a catalogue of the gaucheries committed by the parson during his efforts to rise in the ecclesiastical community.) He had a nephew, he said, who had risen to prominence as an alderman, and with whom he had much influence. The rector had prevailed upon him to use this influence to bring about the election of a candidate favorable to their interests, but Adams (with a curious mixture of idealism and self-interest) refused to do so. As a result, he lost his curacy. Later, convinced of the merits of one Sir Thomas Booby (but also spurred on by the promise of a "living" - i.e. an ecclesiastical position), he interceded with his nephew; the promised living did not materialize, mainly because his dress did not suit the tastes of Lady Booby. Adams has learned that his sermons are quite pleasing to a number of influential persons who might be able to arrange for the ordination of his thirty year old son (yet, in five years, they have not brought it about).

CHAPTER 9

(Adams' discourse on himself considered as a political animal is answered in this chapter by the stranger's speech on "bravery and heroic virtue.") He is outraged by cowardice, and would hang a man that would not die for his country. Adams tries to mollify him, and offers the instance of Hector, who fled from the fray. On their way to the man's house (whither he had invited Adams) he was continuing his discourse on courage, when they overheard the cries of a young woman beset by an attacker. Adams, brandishing his crabstick, rushed to her aid, while the spokesman for courage and noble sacrifice slunk away with a muttered excuse. Adams leveled a blow at the head of the assailant (and Fielding facetiously divagates upon the ingenuity of Nature in creating skulls of a thickness nicely proportioned to the calling of their owners, and then proceeds to describe the quick exchange of two blows in an elaborate Homeric fashion). Getting the worst of it at first, Adams finally emerged victorious, striking a blow which knocked the fellow unconscious (Adams fearful that he had killed him).

CHAPTERS 10 AND 11

Standing over his opponent, and oblivious to the presence of the woman he had rescued, the parson meditated at length on his alternatives-to make his escape, or to deliver himself into the hands of justice.

Comment

The very word "justice," considering the satirical browbeating Fielding has been giving the judicial system, begins to appear ironic whenever it is used. Part of Adams humorousness, however, is that he still naively imagines that ideal justice is available for the asking.

As he stood, a group of bird trappers came up, at which point the rogue on the ground leaped to his feet, accusing Adams and the girl of being in league to rob him; the trappers then took the parson into custody. (We now have another scene in which perjury, circumstantial evidence, greed, and contentiousness all conspire [almost] to bring about a grave miscarriage of justice. Only the purely adventitious presence of Squire Booby, who is able to vouch for Adams, saves his neck. With as minuscule an amount of just evidence as that upon which they were almost convicted, the parson and the girl [it turns out that she is none other than Fanny] are now released.) As Adams and the justice sat discussing the issues that had brought them together, an uproar was heard from without, and it was discovered to have been caused by an argument among those who had apprehended him over whose share of the reward would have been greatest had the parson in fact been convicted. (The report of this ludicrous competition reminds Adams of a similar incident involving two of his clerks, and he remarks philosophically on the folly of heated disputes where neither party has any interest.) Gradually, however, the two men themselves fall into an argument over the question whether the justice ought not in strictness of law to have committed the parson, the justice holding that he should not have done so and Adams maintaining that he should. A heated quarrel would surely have ensued had not Fanny arrived opportunely with word that they were to travel to the very inn at which Joseph was staying.

CHAPTER 12

They had not travelled far when a storm forced them to take shelter at an inn, where they proceeded to warm themselves at the fire. The host, his wife, the maid, and the guide were all impressed with Fanny's beauty (which gives Fielding an opportunity for an unrestrained description of her charms). She was a plump, beautiful young woman, with chestnut hair, high forehead, black sparkling eyes, and a Roman nose-a picture of country charm-with a bashfulness and a natural gentility beyond the acquisition of art.

As they sat, the strains of a song were wafted to them from an inner room. It was a love **ballad**, in which Strephon laments the obduracy of Chloe in a series of romantic cliches; yet it ends in amusingly blunt half-stanza:

Ah, Chloe, expiring, I cried,

How long I thy cruelty bore!

Ah, Strephon, she blushing replied,

You ne'er was so pressing before.

Comment

It is Joseph (as they soon learn) who is singing within, and the pattern of the song-the overcoming of conventional disdain by simple urgency-follows neatly on the heels of the frank, sensuous description of Fanny's attractions, both together introducing a **theme** of artless and sinless love and physical attraction, moving in another dimension from the prurient intrigues and bawdy excursions encountered thus far at the Booby house and the various inns.

Fanny grew pale at the voice, Adams flung his *Aeschylus* into the fire in excitement, and the rest of the inn's inhabitants came running, Joseph among them. He embraced Fanny warmly, and imprinted numberless kisses on her lips, until, recollecting herself, she pushed Joseph gently away.

SUMMARY (CHAPTERS 7-12)

These chapters bring the story to the point at which Joseph and Fanny meet, develop the character of Adams in more detail, and fill out the **themes** of affectation with further incidents, such as the capture and arraignment of Adams on purely circumstantial evidence and the word of an untrustworthy witness.

1. Plot:

The adventitious manner in which Adams meets Fanny, and the stagey scene in which Fanny overhears Joseph singing a **ballad** are additional indications of the small value Fielding attaches to logical necessity, as well as anticipations of the very contrived **denouement** of the novel (in which, for instance, a strawberry mark serves to establish Joseph's identity).

2. Characterization:

   a. New characters:

   (1.) the "man of courage" - an example of the stock dramatic figure of the "braggart soldier" as well as an occasion (so it has been suggested) for Fielding to criticize Tory objections to a standing army and to the lax conduct of the war with Spain.

   (2.) A justice of the peace who is scandalously inept, yet vain over what he considers his "nice discernment."

   (3.) Various minor characters including an ignorant parson and a would-be wit, who challenges Adams to a duel in the quotation of lines of Latin verse.

   b. Adams' character is deepened by further revelations of his quixotic tendencies; when he misses his way at one point, for example, (practically an impossibility for any human creature) Fielding remarks that "he had a wonderful capacity at these kinds of bare possibilities." On the other hand, his commendable willingness to sit down and reason philosophically with any man is shown in his discourses with the "man of courage" and the justice (though his philosophical aplomb does give way, in the latter case, to stubborn argumentativeness).

3. Symbolic details:

   a. Like the Leonora story earlier, the **ballad** sung by Joseph, while superficially irrelevant to the main concerns of the book, does point up subtly the love between Joseph and Fanny, and anticipate its eventual flowering.

   b. It has been noted (by Battestin) that the political discourse by Adams (Chapter 8) may contain a level of topical allegory related to Fielding's disaffection from the Country Party and acceptance of patronage from Walpole, his former political enemy.

CHAPTER 13

Mrs. Slipslop, though she knew Fanny very well, refused to acknowledge her curtsy (standing on her "gentility" once more). This leads Fielding to a lengthy essay on the two sorts of people into which the human species are divided, high people and low people (like Charles Lamb's "Two Races of Men" - borrowers and lenders). High people, he declares, are people of fashion, and low people, people of no fashion. The entire scale of social relationship is passed in review, being referred to by Fielding as "this whole ladder of dependence," all the occupants of which believe it a condescension to speak to persons one step below them, and degradation to go a step further. His digression, Fielding goes on, is merely to vindicate Mrs. Slipslop, since her behavior is quite in accord with common practice.

Adams pursued Mrs. Slipslop into the next room trying to awaken in her memories of Fanny, but that worthy woman dismissed her as an inferior servant, probably a slut, one whose acquaintance Adams would be at some pains to explain. Attempting unsuccessfully to convince Joseph to leave Fanny and accompany her, Slipslop flew into a violent rage, threatened to inform on them to Lady Booby, and made indecent aspersions about the character of the clergy. (As Fielding strongly intimates, Slipslop's conduct is absolutely the result of chagrin and disappointment at finding Joseph alone at first and prey to her designs on his chastity, only to discover later that he was in the company of Fanny and the parson.) The enraged Slipslop departed; Adams, after smoking three pipes, napped in a comfortable chair; and the two young lovers spent the long hours exchanging endearments, "a happiness of which none of my readers who have never been in love are capable of the least conception, though we had as many tongues as Homer desired to describe it with, and which all true lovers will represent to their own minds, without the least assistance from us."

Comment

The drolly witty tone, characteristic of Fielding throughout, should not be allowed to distort his essential sympathy and seriousness at this point. There are times, after all, when hyperboles like "Fanny ... gave up her whole soul to Joseph" are justified by the facts. The author is unquestionably praising the frank and uncomplicated emotion which is theirs.

Awakening the parson summarily, with the expectation that he will marry them forthwith, Joseph is dismayed to discover that Adams rebukes them for wishing to marry without proper publication of the banns. This discouraging news was followed by the presentation of the reckoning, which none of them had money to pay for. Learning that there was a wealthy person in the parish, however, Adams resolved to pay him a visit, confident that he would be only too happy to relieve a brother in want.

CHAPTER 14

Parson Trulliber (for that was his name) was a parson only on Sundays-a farmer the rest of the week. As rotund as Falstaff, loud and hoarse of voice, he spoke with a broad accent and walked like a goose. From Adams' appearance Trulliber and his wife imagined that he had come to buy some hogs, and ushered him unceremoniously into the hog-pen, until Adams cried out in anguish, "Nil habeo cum porcis" (I have nothing to do with hogs). They then sat together at table, Adams thus having ample opportunity to note the man's rudeness, brutality and pride. Still suffering from idealistic outlook, however, Adams optimistically announced his conviction to Trulliber that "you will joyfully embrace such an opportunity of laying up a treasure in a better place than any this world affords," and asked for the loan of fourteen shillings. Reeling in astonishment, Trulliber finally gasped that he knew where to lay up his treasure as well as another, "what matters where a man's treasure is, whose heart is in the Scriptures?" Thinking momentarily that Trulliber was about to grant his request, Adams seized his hand in gratitude, but was soon dispossessed of his naive hope when he heard himself called for a thief and a vagabond. Rebuking Trulliber for his lack of charity, the parson chided: "If you trust to your knowledge for your justification, you will find yourself deceived, though you should add faith to it, without good works."

Comment

The reference to knowledge, of course, is to Trulliber's claim that "his heart is in the Scriptures." Adams means that Trulliber has no more hope of salvation on that principle than those contemporary sects who preach that faith alone, without good works, is sufficient to be saved. There is perhaps a tinge of **irony** in the fact that Adams, good man though he is, seems doomed to the loss of earthly salvation because of his reliance on knowledge (his *Aeschylus,* and the ancient philosophers) rather than experience.

After an exchange of angry words, Adams took his leave.

CHAPTER 15

Adams returned to the inn, and the friends agreed that the only recourse was to ask the hostess to trust them. Surprisingly, she agreed at once (thinking from Adams' earlier remark that he was a natural brother, rather than an ecclesiastical one, to Trulliber, and fearing the consequences of her refusal). Adams having left his great coat at Trulliber's, however, the hostess offered to procure it, where she was of course disabused of her erroneous belief concerning their relationship, and returned more insistent than ever that they pay the reckoning. After several other unsuccessful forays about the parish, the parson was about to give up, when an itinerant peddler, hearing of their distress, readily gave them his last six shillings and sixpence, to which Adams added a sixpence, making up their total bill.

CHAPTER 16

About two miles further on, the three friends encountered a friendly fellow seated at an alehouse door, who invited them to conversation and a repast. After an exchange of ideas and sentiments, the gentleman, who gave every evidence of being a rich man, professed himself delighted with Adams' character and address and offered him the parish living (three hundred pounds a year), and a house and grounds. For the present he would arrange to have them put up, and would send his coach and six to take them the rest of their journey. Overwhelmed, but absolutely convinced of the man's sincerity, Adams blessed him for his "primitive Christian charity." After his departure, the three waited for the gentleman's promises to materialize, only to discover through vain messages and emissaries that he had no intention of making good on them-that it was in fact a bizarre sort of practical joke. The host of the alehouse, who had kept silent throughout out of natural reticence, confirmed the melancholy fact, but refused to demand payment for their sustenance and insisted on their tarrying for at least another pot of ale at his expense. Adams avowed himself happy to find at least one Christian in a country which he had come to believe inhabited only by Turks.

CHAPTER 17

The host assured Adams that he was not the first to have been taken in by the mendacious squire, and acquainted him with the cases of an aspiring exciseman, who had been at considerable expense to qualify himself for a place promised him by the squire, a young man whose father put him through school on the squire's promise that he would maintain him at the university, and a young woman whom he had enticed to London with the promise of being made a gentlewoman to a lady of quality. All had been disappointed, the first ending his days in prison, the second dying of grief and alcoholic consumption, and the young woman turning to the life of a common whore. Even the host himself had suffered at his hands. Once the master of a ship which had been captured, he was promised the lieutenancy of a man-of-war, being assured by the squire that he was promoting his interest at the admiralty office. Only by chance did he learn that his name had never been brought before the board, at which point he decided to set up as keeper of an alehouse. "May the squire," he declared, "and all such sneaking rascals, go to the devil together."

The good parson admonished the host for this sentiment, confessing that though he conceded the squire's wickedness, he yet found symptoms in his countenance of that "sweetness of disposition" which makes a good Christian. The host derided Adams' penchant for physiognomy, whereupon the parson defended his viewpoint by opposing his "travels" through the world of books to the host's sea voyages, and asserting that there was ample warrant in books for the science of physiognomy, notably the story of Socrates, who exonerated a physiognomist who had detected a vicious tendency in his character from the charge of charlatanism by admitting that he did indeed possess those traits, having overcome them only by the force of his will. (Adams' defense of books and the hosts of practical experience bids fair to become an open quarrel, when the timely arrival of Joseph and Fanny, pressing for the parson's departure, brings it to an end. Together, they renew their journey.)

SUMMARY (CHAPTERS 13-17)

These chapters bring the second book to a close, though it can hardly be said that there is any finality about them. We are given some further insight into the incredible extent of Adams' gullibility, presented with a few character types whose vices are unusual enough to spark new interest, and reminded of the principle thread of the narrative by the appearance of Slipslop and her designs on Joseph.

1. Adams' naivete now takes the forms of:

    a. Imagining that, in the name of clerical brotherhood, he has a claim on the charity of a local wealthy parson.

    b. Believing the outrageous promises of a house and living made to him by a squire with whom he has just struck up a bare acquaintance.

    c. Attempting to vindicate the character of an abandoned wretch in the opinion of a hard-hearted tavern keeper by invoking the authority of books, especially the ancient classics.

2. Important new characters:

    a. Parson Trulliber-a boorish, selfish un-Christian cleric.

    b. An unnamed squire who is a pathological liar, and who satisfies his ego by making fantastic promises which he is unable to keep.

c. A tavern keeper, applauded by Adams for his Christian charity when he refuses to accept payment from them, but condemned by the parson when he refuses to believe that there is a reclaimable Christian soul lurking in the depths of the being of the mendacious squire.

3. Continued themes:

   a. The works vs. faith controversy (in the Trulliber **episode**).

   b. The operation of vanity and hypocrisy (especially in the incident of the squire's promises).

4. The structure of the work can be seen ever more clearly to reside in parallels of character and incident, there being only superficial and accidental differences between the monstrous examples of depravity that Adams encounters. The reader's main interest is centered in the character of Adams; how long can he maintain his sanguine view of human nature and preserve his own Christian and stoic outlook in the face of the trials he encounters? Of course, Fielding is too good an artist not to provide continuing references to the story line, in such **episodes** as the confrontation of Slipslop and Fanny, with its implications for the Slipslop-Lady Booby-Joseph affair.

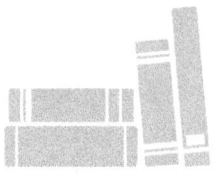

JOSEPH ANDREWS

TEXTUAL ANALYSIS

BOOK III

CHAPTER 1

This first chapter is not a narrative but an **exposition** of Fielding's theory of the novel. He makes the following points:

1. He is concerned not with fact but with truth - not with the historically actual but with the humanly probable. His characters are to convince readers of their reality without having to be certified as actually existent individuals.

2. His work is a history-history in the sense that it is a true copy of Nature rather than an original created from a "confused heap of matter" in a writer's brain.

Comment

Whether he recognizes the debt or not, Fielding closely follows a number of principles laid down by Aristotle in his Poetics. Aristotle, of course, regarded the truth of poetry as superior to the truth of history, and placed much emphasis on the mimetic (that is, imitative) quality of literature. In his famous definition of tragedy, Aristotle began by calling it "an imitation of an action."

3. He intends to "describe not men, but manners; not an individual but a species."

4. He is writing comedy, that is, a work which enables readers to see their own deformities writ large, and thus be able by suffering private mortification to avoid public shame.

Comment

This therapeutic theory of comedy is in the tradition of English stage comedy going back to Ben Jonson, and ultimately to classical theory, particularly as expressed by Horace in his *Ars Poetica*, wherein he enunciates the famous principle, "He [that is, the author] takes every vote, who mixes the useful with the sweet." A good deal of eighteenth-century literature, in fact, was written more or less explicitly in accordance with this principle.

CHAPTER 2

As the three friends rested under the pitch black sky, a light appeared in the distance, and then vanished, a circumstance which caused Adams to suspect the presence of ghosts and to discourse at some length about their properties. The lights, however, soon proved to be human creatures (murderers, as it seemed from their conversation), and the travellers huddled together to escape them. They would undoubtedly have gone unnoticed had not Adams, who had just assured his companions that he despised death as much as any man, felt compelled to quote aloud a **couplet** from the *Aeneid,* which expressed his thoughts exactly. Only Joseph's sensible intervention allowed them to escape without detection. (Joseph, indeed, begins to assume more and more the role of guide and protector. Adams tumbles down a hill, but Joseph carries Fanny down in his arms. Adams wishes to wade through a stream, but Joseph sensibly advises him to walk along the bank, where they will surely find a ford or bridge.

Comment

One of the central critical problems connected with *Joseph Andrews* is just this matter of the centrality of Joseph in the plot of the work, and the consistency with which Fielding presents his character. Recent opinion inclines to regard him as at least as important as Adams, and as undergoing a development of character towards assurance and maturity.

Coming to a cottage standing near an orchard, they knocked at the door and were admitted by a very pleasant gentleman and his charming wife, who gave them refreshments, and conversed very civilly. Adams and the man fell into a discussion of the peculiar merits of Homer, the parson launching into what is practically a synopsis of the Iliad, and registering his reaction to each **episode**. The gentleman's suspicions that Fanny was the daughter of some person of fashion, that Joseph had run away with her, and that Adams had connived at it, were allayed by the open, genial conduct of his guests, and he quickly became enamored of them all, offering to tell them the history of his life.

CHAPTER 3

(The gentleman's name is Wilson, and though none of them is aware of it, he is actually Joseph's father, the revelation of which brings about the final **denouement** of the novel.) He was descended from a good family, left school around the age of seventeen, and sought his fortune in London. He found it easy to acquire a reputation as a fine gentleman, quickly learning all the fashionable accomplishments, becoming privy to the open secrets of the beau monde, and getting a reputation for being involved in intrigues with half a dozen women of the town. His days were spent entirely in dressing, walking, dining, and attending coffee-houses and theatres. This life was cut short only by Wilson's gaining a reputation for cowardice by taking an insult without offering a challenge to a duel. He next took quarters in another section of town, amidst another class of people, but found that their routine was as vain as the former, though he now descended to the depth of visiting whores and making love to orange-wenches. Next, he kept a mistress, and proceeded from this to ruining by his debauchery a match between a fine young woman and an apprentice with whom she was in love, first spoiling her reputation and then her character, until she ran off to become a prostitute, ending her days in Newgate prison. Then he became involved with Sapphira, the wife of a man of fashion and a notorious coquette. (Fielding has Adams express his ignorance of this term, and has Wilson describe a coquette at great length, as if it were some kind of oddity in the field of natural history. The description bears favorable comparison with Addison's famous "Dissection of a Coquette's Heart.") Ultimately getting nowhere with the coquette, whose heart was too unfixed to settle on any one man, he next alienated the affections of the wife of a decent citizen, was found out and sued for three thousand pounds, ending with a severe blow to his fortune and the man's wife on his hands.

From love-making, he went to the society of drinking men, thence to the playhouses and the parties conducted by actors. Only at this point was he able to formulate for himself the moral principle that "vanity is the worst of passions." Adams interrupted, fumbling in his pockets for a sermon on vanity of which he was quite proud, but discovered that he had mislaid it. Said Adams, "I would read it, for I am confident you would admire it: indeed, I have never been a greater enemy to any passion, than that silly one of vanity."

Comment

Fielding obviously expects his readers to be amused by the fact that Adams is unwittingly convicting himself of having some degree of that very vanity he inveighs against.

From actors Wilson proceeded to gamesters, by whom he was quickly impoverished, and finding himself destitute, resolved to write plays for money, and found himself caught up in the wretched machinery of patronage, forced to beg from his friends and spend hours and days waiting at the doors of rich men. The production of his first play was delayed so long that, in despair, he had to turn to hack writing for the lawyers, and then to translating for a bookseller, until, too weak to continue, he found himself arrested for debt. In his extremity, a friend arrived with the good news that a lottery ticket Wilson had purchased had won the prize of three thousand pounds, but finding out that he had sold the ticket two days before, the friend began to revile him in the most violent manner.

Suddenly, in these desperate circumstances, Wilson received a letter from the daughter of the man who had bought the lottery ticket, (and, opportunely, had just died), offering sympathy and a banknote for two hundred pounds. No sooner did Wilson pay his debts and provide himself with a new wardrobe than he paid a visit to this angel of mercy (Harriet Hearty by name) and discovered her to be the divinest creature he had ever seen. Her beauty, kindness, and charity so overwhelmed him that he followed protestations of love with urgent importunities that another woman might have used as an excuse to dismiss him from her life. Harriet, however, employed such gentility and understanding, even while she refused him any undeserved familiarities, that their love prospered and resulted in marriage. After a short, unsuccessful venture into the wine business with her fortune of six thousand pounds, they retired together into the country "from a world full of bustle, noise, hatred, envy, and ingratitude, to ease, quiet, and love." The only misfortune they had since suffered was the loss of their three year old son, stolen by gypsies (Joseph, of course, though the fact is still unknown to them).

Comment

Behind the obvious exaggerations in Wilson's account, it is clear that Fielding's close familiarity with fashionable London society and the world of the theater (since he was himself a playwright) had given him much solid substance for **satire**. Indeed, the only exaggeration is in the fact that all of these adventures are represented as having occurred to a single individual.

CHAPTER 4

After informing Adams that his lost son could be identified by a strawberry mark on his left breast, Wilson took him on a tour of the garden. Though plainly ornamented, there was abundant variety of fruit and vegetables, tended by Wilson himself, usually beginning early in the morning while his wife was caring for the children and preparing the breakfast. He spent much time with his wife, for he did not agree with the popular notion that women were inferior to men in understanding.

Comment

Fielding steers a middle course here between the (Platonic) notion that women are intellectual inferiors to men, as Donne, for instance, expresses it:

> Hope not for mind in women, at their best Sweetness and wit, they are but Mummy, possess't.

and the popular (Bluestocking) movement to allow women to take their places as man's political, intellectual, and social equals. The reactionary view is amusingly presented in Boswell's prodding of Johnson into going to hear a woman preacher, just to note his reaction. Said Johnson, "It is like a dog walking on its hind legs; one marvels not that the thing is done well or poorly, but that it is done at all." Fielding (if we may assume that Wilson's view is his own) believes that no men are "capable of making juster observations on life, or of delivering them more agreeably."

Adams remarking that the sometimes regretted his wife's ignorance of Greek, Wilson was quick to point out that his own wife's arts were purely of the domestic sort, and that he was careful to rear his daughters with strict limitations on their knowledge of books and the world so that they should never be bred above the rank they might someday occupy, nor despise a plain husband if that should be their lot. (This is plainly a picture of the "good life" - the wholesome influence of the country, and nature, on naturally well-disposed minds. As the travellers left, Adams declared that this was the way people lived in the Golden Age.)

CHAPTER 5

After lengthy meditation Adams burst out with the opinion that the cause of all the gentleman's calamities was his attendance at a " public school" (schools like Eton-what we should call a "private school"). They were breeding grounds of immorality and vice. Joseph, with surprising truculence (more evidence of his growth in independence) demurred, asserting that a person of "righteous temper" could be corrupted by no school, not even by residence in London. Adams chided him for his forwardness, and ran on in the same vein until they arrived at a beautiful spot of ground, whose features no art or paint could reproduce, and refreshed themselves with the provisions that Wilson had given them.

Comment

Pictures of idyllic simplicity become more and more frequent as they continue deeper into the country world and leave London farther behind.

BRIGHT NOTES STUDY GUIDE

CHAPTER 6

(Paralleling Adams' speech on schools, is a lengthy reflection by Joseph on charity and good works, alleging his puzzlement at the fact that people are so prone to praise good works but not to perform them, and to condemn the very vices they constantly seek to practice.) Fanny asked Joseph if all great men were wicked, to which he replied that he had heard of a few good men, one in particular noted for his charitable foundations. Adams, through all this, was snoring loudly, which gave the lovers the opportunity for some innocent dalliance, interrupted, however, by the arrival of a pack of hounds chasing an unfortunate hare (a sight which moved the tender emotions of Fanny). The dogs, in killing their prey, became tangled in Adams' cassock, whereupon he awakened suddenly and fled, leaving a third of his cassock behind. The master of the hunt, coming up and taking in the situation at a glance, was not the least bit averse to hunting men as well as hares, and cried out upon the hounds to pursue the fleeing parson.

Comment

The mock-heroic aspects of the novel reach their **climax** in this scene, in which Joseph seizes his cudgel (which is described in grandiloquent terms) and beats down some of the dogs, Adams lays about him with his crabstick, felling the enemy in droves, and the hunting squire and his friends stand by laughing at the scene. The language is in the Homeric vein, with occasional interruptions by Fielding to apologize for the fact that he has failed to include a heroic **simile**, or for some other imagined deficiency of style.

The squire finally called off his dogs, and with a great show of apology (though it was plain that he had enjoyed their discomfiture hugely) insisted that all share his hospitality at his house. Reluctantly the three friends agreed to accompany him.

CHAPTER 7

The squire took the precaution of ordering his servants to get Joseph and Adams drunk, so that he might work his will on Fanny, a design which had been in his mind all along. He was a bachelor, forty years of age, who had been a libertine from the earliest age, corrupting even his tutor. After a European tour, when merely confirmed him in vice, he returned home to a seat in parliament, and surrounded himself with all things "ridiculous, odious, and absurd in his own species." He was, in short, surrounded by curs, both of the canine and human sort, who sought to please him by outdoing one another in practical jokes. One pulled Adams chair out from under him; another poured soup in his lap; a third (a poet) made satirical verses about him. When a firecracker exploded beneath him, Adams decided he had had enough, and rose to his feet, making a lengthy speech rebuking the squire for his coarseness and inhospitality, and offering to thrash a captain who had insulted him. With feigned gravity, the gentleman apologized, but at the prompting of a doctor in the company, arranged a final trick which was to cause Adams a dunking, which indeed it did, though the parson had the satisfaction of pulling the squire in with him and sousing him two or three times.

SUMMARY (CHAPTERS 1 - 7)

The opening chapters of the third book are noteworthy for the development of the character of Joseph, the complication of plot represented by the introduction of Wilson (Joseph's father) and the emergence of a more positive - and romantic - theme.

1. There are several occasions on which Joseph's growing independence brings him into conflict with Adams:

   a. His decision to walk along the river bank in search of a bridge, rather than wade across as Adams wishes.

   b. His restraining of Adams from sallying forth to whip the young squire who shot Wilson's daughter's dog.

   c. His disagreement with Adams (here it is intellectual independence) in his belief that public schools are the chief nurses of vice.

2. The idyllic happiness which Joseph and Fanny now enjoy increases apprehension that some malign force will intervene to ruin it-that is, there is a building up of suspense as to the outcome of their quest. This suspense is complicated by the introduction of Wilson and the story of his lost son, with the strawberry mark on his breast.

3. Among the new characters introduced are:

   a. Wilson-a gentleman who, from a life of profligacy in the city, has turned with the aid of a loving wife to a life of domestic bliss in the country.

b. A squire whose chief delight in life is the playing of cruel practical jokes-he is a libertine, coarse and sensual, and surrounded by a pack of fawning hangerson.

4. The story of Wilson's life and the scenes of country beauty which the travellers happen upon point up the **theme** of city vice vs. country virtue. But it is by no means that simple an affair; Fielding includes the **episode** of the cruel squire partly as an indication that residence in the country is no guarantee of moral behavior. The individual, after all, must cooperate with grace.

CHAPTER 8

The three travellers made seven miles in great haste, stopping at an alehouse called the New Inn. As they sat at leisure after a supper of bread, cheese, and ale, and Adams thanked God for their sustenance more than if it had been a splendid dinner, a certain grave stranger entered upon a long discourse on the **theme** of the contempt of wealth, which caused Adams to inquire if he were not a clergyman. (Though he denies it, Fielding informs us in an aside that he is indeed a priest of the Church of Rome.)

Comment

The Roman Catholic Church still enjoyed the reputation in England of being a hotbed of luxury, and the **irony** of a Catholic priest declaiming about the contempt of wealth, would not have been lost on an eighteenth-century reader.

When he has finished, the stranger begs eighteen pence of Adams with which to pay his bill; Adams offers to share with him the half guinea he owns, but fumbling in his pocket discovers that it has been picked by the squire's henchmen. The priest sarcastically accuses him of lying, and after begging the host to trust him for the amount departs, "not without confusion." (The entire situation is of course deliciously ironic, with the two clergymen, who do not have a penny between them, loudly expostulating about the corrupting influence of money.) The travellers retired to "homely beds," in which "health and fatigue gave them a sweeter repose than is often in the power of velvet and down to bestow" (another suggestion of the purity to be found in rural surroundings).

CHAPTER 9

In the morning, the squire's minions arrived at the inn demanding admittance so that they might carry Fanny back to the squire's house, since she was undoubtedly being kidnapped by the two men who accompanied her. The host admitted them, and all-the captain, the poet, the player, and three other servants-fell upon them, the captain bidding defiance to gunpowder (when he was assured they had no firearms), the poet retreating downstairs prudently, saying it was "his business to record great actions, and not to do them." At first, Joseph and Adams had the better of it, the parson giving the captain a violent blow, and Joseph hurling a huge stone chamber pot and its contents at his face. Numbers, however, finally told, and Joseph was laid low and Adams securely held, Fanny being carried off on the player's horse, while her two friends were secured back to back to the bed-post.

CHAPTER 10

(This chapter is, in Fielding's words, "a discourse between the poet and the player; of no other use in this history but to divert the reader.") They begin by complimenting each other on their professions and decrying their own. The poet accuses contemporary playwrights of writing such bad speeches that not even the greatest of actors could do them justice, and the player replies that actors nowadays are so poor that they are never equal to the delicacy of sentiment and the subtle emphases the poets have provided. They soon reverse positions, however, when the poet asks the player to repeat a speech he had written for him in a recent play, and he claims to have forgotten it. The player claims that it was loudly hissed during the performance, the poet that it was the declamation, not the speech itself, that was hissed. (In another aside, Fielding remarks that their discourse was ended by an accident that the impatient reader must skip the next chapter to discover.)

CHAPTER 11

When Joseph recovered his senses he fell to grieving aloud for the loss of the sweet object of his love, and shed many tears and uttered many groans over his plight. Adams, in a bumbling effort to console him, began to remind Joseph of his duty as a Christian to accept any trial which might come his way. What though he has lost "the kindest, loveliest, sweetest young woman," who would have been the delight of his youth and the comfort of his age; what though she will probably be ravished by a lustful villain; all things happen by Divine permission, and we should not repine at our fate. Furthermore, these trials may be punishments for our sins, and in any case we have no power to thwart them. Joseph admitted the truth of Adams' remarks, but alleged that they had no power to assuage his grief. "Tell me," cries Joseph, "that Fanny will escape back to my arms." But Adams continued with his counsels of fortitude, until Joseph burst out with the following speech (from *Macbeth*):

Yes, I will bear my sorrows like a man, But I must also feel them like a man. I cannot but remember such things were, And were most dear to me.

Comment

Adams' counsels of sweet reasonableness, based on the stoic philosophy so dear to him, obviously have no power to alter the existential fact of grief. All the "consolations of philosophy" ever written address themselves only to the rationalizing mind, to the utter neglect of the fact of man's human feelings. The quotation from Shakespeare is the ultimate reply to Adams' advice.

CHAPTER 12

As the captain rode along with his prize he attempted to persuade her to yield her favors willingly to the squire, inasmuch as there was no hope of escape and the squire would be much more kindly disposed towards her if he did not have to use force. But Fanny regarded him not, and merely cried out loudly to heaven for assistance despite the captain's threats to stop her mouth. A horseman appeared, and Fanny called for assistance, but the captain maintained that he was carrying his wife home from an assignation with an adulterer. Two more horsemen then came into sight, and one of them recognizing her as Fanny Goodwill, they seized the captain and freed the young woman. The chariot upon which they were attending soon drove up, and was discovered by Fanny to contain none other than Peter Pounce, who was preceding Lady Booby by only a few miles. When they returned to the inn, the poet and player fled for their lives, and Joseph ran directly to the captain with a challenge to a fight, which the captain, however, refused. The lad then administered a severe drubbing to him with a cudgel. The mistress of the house, berating her husband for a blockhead and a numbskull, pleaded with Pounce to be lenient with her; since Adams was inclined to forgive them, she was released. With a good deal of discussion and mild argument (since Pounce would have liked to have Fanny in the chariot with him, and Adams wanted to walk and leave his horse to Joseph and Fanny), the travelling accommodations were finally decided, with Pounce and Adams taking the chariot, and Joseph and Fanny riding on a horse belonging to one of her rescuers, while he rode on Adams' horse, the whole procession then setting out for Booby Hall.

CHAPTER 13

An innocent remark of Adams about some beautiful prospects (landscapes) he had seen, caused Pounce to mention his own lands, and Adams to counter by saying that "riches without charity were nothing worth." They have different notions of charity, said Peter, calling it a "mean, parson-like quality"; Adams replied that it was "a generous disposition to relieve the distressed," whereupon Pounce delivered himself of the opinion that human distress was mostly imaginary, cold and nakedness, for instance, being evils introduced by "luxury and custom." (By degrees, Pounce moves from statements about how poor he actually is, largely as a result of taxation, to prideful comments about his status as a self-made man and the great extent of his wealth. He finally makes bluntly derogatory remarks about Adams' appearance, congratulating himself on having such a good nature that he even suffers him to ride in the same chariot. Finally stung by Pounce's insults, the parson leaps out of the chariot and walks the rest of the way.)

SUMMARY (CHAPTERS 8-13)

These chapters are the means of returning to the main plot line, with the appearance of Peter Pounce and the information that Lady Booby is not far behind. In addition:

1. Fielding introduces the characters of:

    a. A Roman Catholic priest, who condemns wealth (doubly ironic, because of popular identification of the Church with wealth, and because he happens actually to be indigent).

    b. A poet and player, who discourse on the relative merits of actors and playwrights in a manner which probably has some topical significance, but which, in terms of the structure of the book, balances the following dialogue (on resignation to the will of God) between Adams and Joseph.

2. The genuineness (and the deep pleasure) of the love between Joseph and Fanny is underscored by the speech Joseph utters while tied to the bedpost, and that which Fanny gives vent to while she is being abducted, as well as by explicit statements of Fielding, such as his declaration: "Let the hard-hearted villain know this, that there is a pleasure in

a tender sensation beyond any which he is capable of tasting:"

3. Adams continues to appear in his double guise of nobility and gaucheness (though Joseph, happily, is able to reject the more impractical side of his influence). His stoic advice to Joseph is ideally above criticism, but in a practical way impossible of attainment. Yet his ideals of Christian charity are impaired not at all from the criticism they suffer at the hands of Pounce, and his leap from Pounce's chariot is a magnificent gesture (only slightly tarnished by Fielding's sly comment that only a mile remained of the trip to Booby Hall).

4. The practically unrelieved catalogue of knaves which makes up the first part of the book is being offset in this section by more frequent appearances of charitable figures, such, for instance, as the horseman who rescues Fanny.

5. Major **themes** are given new emphasis and prominence:

    a. The meaning of charity (in the argument between Pounce and Adams).

    b. The ultimate triumph of the "gentle heart" (Fanny's timely rescue).

    c. The goodness and wholesomeness of rustic surroundings (the power of plain bread and cheese to refresh, and the superiority of Adams' homely bed to "velvet and down").

JOSEPH ANDREWS

TEXTUAL ANALYSIS

BOOK IV

CHAPTER 1

Lady Booby arrived back in the village simultaneously with the other travellers, and, noticing Joseph in their midst, alternately blanched and flushed. The villagers were indeed happy to see her, since their livelihood depended entirely on the monies which her presence diverted to their coffers, but much more genuinely happy to see Parson Adams, who went from one to the other with fond personal greetings. Joseph and Fanny too were warmly welcomed. (Most of the chapter is now taken up with a flashback to Lady Booby's London house just after her dismissal of Joseph, and recounts repetitively her rages, ardors, and speculations centering about the person of Joseph-how she tried to demean him in her own opinion, how she berated Slipslop for having induced her to dismiss him, and how, despite all protestations to the contrary, she found herself still in the grips of an overriding passion for him.) On Sunday, the morning after her arrival in the village, she attended church, where her eyes were frequently on Joseph, until she heard Adams announce the banns of marriage between Joseph Andrews and Frances Goodwill, after which she glanced around angrily. As soon as she returned home she sent for Adams.

CHAPTER 2

When Adams entered Lady Booby's presence she accused him of perpetrating a monstrous thing, by trying to procure a match between Joseph and Fanny, an idle fellow and a wench. Adams, however, stoutly defended his actions and their characters. Fanny was not only sweet and honest, but beautiful, and Joseph had a legal right (having been settled for a year) to marry in the parish. To Lady Booby's complaint that she did not wish the village populated with vagabonds and beggars, Adams retorted that to be poor was no crime and that it would be barbarous to forbid them to marry. She then threatened him with dismissal from his cure if he should continue to publish the banns, and warned that her doors would be closed to him. Adams proudly replied that he entered no doors where he was not welcome, and that the justice of his actions would finally become evident.

Comment

This is easily Adams' most impressive scene so far. All of his hauteur, idealism, obstinacy, and pride, which on other occasions have made him appear somewhat ridiculous, here raise him to magnificent stature. Even without knowledge of Lady Booby's ulterior motives, his reason and compassion, and willingness to suffer utterly vanquish her. He is most heroic at this instant of confrontation with a paragon of fashionable pretense and hypocrisy-far more than when he is cracking heads or fighting off dogs.

CHAPTER 3 AND 4

Lawyer Scout having been summoned by Lady Booby, he denied having interfered with her conduct of her servants' affairs. He had given Adams the information about a year's settlement merely in a passing way. In any case, there was a legal difference between "settled in law" and "settled in fact," and he would have no difficulty in proving the case against young Andrews. As for the wench, she was no beauty, but an ugly creature, who well deserved to be forbidden to marry. The parson, Scout was sure, was concerned only for his fee, and could easily be taken care of. "The laws of this land are not so vulgar, to permit a mean fellow to contend with one of your ladyship's fortune." If he were to be dragged before Judge Frolick, he would be committed, and there would be an end of it. (Scout, Fielding explains in an addendum to the chapter, was one of those "pests of society" who, without any training in the law, take it upon themselves to act as lawyers, in clear defiance of an act of parliament.)

Lady Booby, attending church the following Tuesday, which was a holiday, heard Parson Adams publish the banns again in as audible a tone as before. She returned home to vent her rage, and was accosted by Slipslop with the news the Joseph and Fanny had been dragged before the justice by Scout. This news, indeed, was hardly pleasing to Lady Booby, since although she cared not at all about Fanny, she was not inclined to have Joseph pass out of her life. At this juncture, her nephew arrived with his wife to the consternation of the great lady, since she had no knowledge that he had ever married. He entered the room saying "Madam, this is that charming Pamela, of whom I am convinced you have heard so much."

> Comment

This is of course the Pamela of Richardson's novel, Lady Booby's nephew being her master Mr. Booby, whom she has finally married.

    Lady Booby received her with civility, and a short while after Mr. Booby, upon being given a whispered message, left on "some business of consequence."

CHAPTER 5

Mr. Booby's business was to repair to the justice's house, where, he had been informed, Pamela's brother was being arraigned. Since he was acquainted with the justice, he took advantage of the fact to inquire concerning the charges against Joseph and Fanny. The justice handed him an illiterate deposition written in his own hand, amounting in the last analysis to the charge that they had broken off a twig belonging to lawyer Scout. The justice was about to commit them to Bridewell for a month. At Mr. Booby's request, they were released in his custody, Joseph being given a suit of his clothes to dress himself in so that he might appear in a favorable light before Pamela's new relatives. As all there were driving back to Lady Booby's they spied Adams walking through a field and prevailed upon him to join them in the coach, acquainting him with the happy turn of events which had just occurred. Upon their arrival, Mr. Booby entered first to request his aunt to accept Joseph and Fanny in her house because of their relationship to Pamela, whose relatives he confessed an obligation to treat with respect. Lady Booby acquiesced in the case of Joseph, but refused absolutely to countenance the presence of Fanny under her roof. Joseph agreeing to see his sister alone, Fanny was sent off in the care of Parson Adams.

CHAPTER 6

The meeting between Joseph and Pamela was attended by tears of joy, and when emotions had subsided Joseph entertained the company with a recital of his adventures (during which Lady Booby ill-concealed her dissatisfaction at those parts involving Fanny). Since she had ordered a bed for Mr. Joseph, he was prevailed upon by all to spend the night, even though he had promised Fanny to return to her that evening. In the morning, however, he rose early and visited the delight of his soul, spending two hours with her in a condition of inexpressible happiness, during which they appointed the following Monday for the wedding.

Lady Booby, upon retiring, had called Slipslop to her and asked for her opinion of Fanny (suitably vile, when she realized the tack her mistress wished her to take) and of Joseph. (They vie with each other in cataloguing Joseph's abilities and charms; at last discussing his superb suitability to be the mate even of a lady of quality, until Slipslop makes the mistake of insinuating that Lady Booby herself should have no misgivings about considering marriage with him. Though her mistress denies that such a thought has ever entered her mind, Slipslop continues her praise of Joseph and then suggests how easy it would be to have Fanny sent packing by Lawyer Scout. Lady Booby of course professes astonishment that Slipslop should imagine that she would ever countenance a move of this sort.) Her ladyship, realizing that she had allowed Slipslop to become too intimate with her began to abuse her as a coarse creature and a "reptile of a lower order," though she finally softened her tone and calling her a "comical creature" bid her good-night.

CHAPTER 7

(Fielding begins this chapter with an essay on feminine disdain. Being instructed from the very earliest age that men are monsters, eager to devour them, young ladies practice a studious antipathy to all men of their acquaintance. At the age of fourteen or fifteen when they notice master's eyes regarding them so earnestly, they believe their only method of salvation is to render themselves amiable in his eyes; later, when they are treated with the utmost fondness and tenderness, and fall in love with the monster, they have practiced deceit so long that they at length impose upon themselves and really believe that they hate what in fact they love.) So it was with Lady Booby, who loved Joseph long before she knew it, until a dream betrayed her true feelings. She then prevailed upon her nephew to persuade Joseph to abandon his intention of marrying Fanny, a task, however, in which he had no success. Unable to convince the youth that he would degrade himself by such a match. Booby declared that he would break the heart of his parents, who now expected to see him rise in the world. Joseph's reply, since it is an excellent illustration of his maturity and independence of mind, is worth quoting:

I know not that my parents have any power over my inclinations: nor am I obliged to sacrifice my happiness to their whim or ambition: besides, I shall be very sorry to see, that the unexpected advancement of my sister should so suddenly inspire them with this wicked pride, and make them despise their equals. I am resolved on no account to quit my dear Fanny;

no, though I could raise her as high above her present station as you have raised my sister . . . all my pleasure is centered in Fanny; and whilst I have health, I shall be able to support her with my labour in that station to which she was born, and with which she is content.

Comment

This is Joseph's moment of magnificence, corresponding to Adams' disdainful rejection of Lady Booby's threats. As in the case of Adams, we find that all the earlier instances of integrity and even stiff-necked pride which had a tendency to appear incredible (and even ridiculous flower in this fine expression of love and principle.

As Fanny was walking some distance from Adams' house, she was set upon by a coarse young gentleman, who attempted to kiss her, and take other liberties. Failing in this, he left his servant behind with orders to exercise all persuasions in his behalf. The man, however, overcome by Fanny's charms, decided to take his will of her and was using violence to this end when Joseph happened along, and administered a sound thrashing to the fellow. In the melee Fanny's handkerchief had been torn from her bosom, and quite involuntarily Joseph found himself staring for some moments at her incomparably white neck, until blushes by both caused him to remove his eyes, "so truly did his passion for her deserve the noble name of love."

CHAPTER 8

Crossing two or three fields, the lovers came to the house of Adams, who no sooner heard that Fanny had eaten no breakfast than he gave her a bone of bacon he had been gnawing on-the last morsel in the house. Joseph acquainted the parson with all that had transpired, and begged that he might be allowed to fetch a license, since he would not draw an easy breath until Fanny should be totally his. Adams then reminded the young man that his desire for haste was either the result of impatience or of fear: if impatience, then as a good Christian he must be admonished to put aside the lusts of the flesh; if fear, then he must be instructed in the necessity of resignation to the will of God, no matter what accident might befall him. Did Abraham refuse to sacrifice Isaac? No Christian ought to set his heart so firmly on any human creature. At that very moment, a messenger arrived to inform Adams that his youngest son had just been drowned, at which news the parson began to stamp about the room and deplore his loss bitterly, Joseph employing (to no avail) the very same arguments which Adams himself had invoked only moments before. As he sallied out the front door, however, he met his son, wet but very much alive, and was immediately conveyed into transports of joy. Both his own involuntary example, and the testimony of Mrs. Adams to the fact that the parson had himself been a very loving husband, overbore poor Adams.

SUMMARY (CHAPTERS 1-8)

The story is fast rising to its **climax**, as all important parties arrive back at the village in which Booby Hall is located. There is a far greater degree of logical connection between episodes, and of purposeful, significant action than heretofore. Chief developments:

1. Plot: Lady Booby tries to separate Joseph and Fanny on a trumped-up charge of theft; her nephew

Mr. Booby (arriving with his wife Pamela) saves them from a prison sentence, but also tries to persuade Joseph not to marry Fanny. Threats to Fanny's unsullied virtue seem to be multiplying, and Joseph's haste in trying to marry her before some **catastrophe** should occur is regarded by Adams as precipitate and un-Christian, though the force of his argument is blunted by his own capitulation to a passionate outburst of grief.

1. New Characters:

    a. Lawyer Scout-a disreputable, time-serving tool of Lady Booby.

    b. Mr. Booby and Pamela - taken from Richardson's *Pamela*, though Booby seems innocuous in his actions here, and Pamela (except for a predictably vulgar air of superiority) is pleasant enough.

2. Adams' character: It is seen at its best in his heroic confrontation with Lady Booby, though his idealism comes under fire once more in the **episode** of the report of his son's drowning.

3. Joseph's character: Joseph has been steadily gaining in maturity and independence. Furthermore, the fact that his "chastity" is not some sort of neurotic withdrawal - and not a subject for ridicule-is established clearly in the incident where his physical passion is aroused by the sight of Fanny's pure white neck. Joseph has, in fact, been manifesting a control over his appetites in a very realistic way (as opposed to Adams' constant stoic prescriptions for virtue).

He comes to seem far more human than Adams as the book nears its close.

CHAPTER 9

Having been informed by her visitor, Beau Didapper (for such was the name of the young gentleman who had most recently assaulted Fanny), of the young beauty he had spied nearby, Lady Booby decided to use him to alienate Fanny's affections from Joseph, and took him with her to the parsonage.

Comment

Didapper is the typical empty-headed, vain, corrupt, court gadfly so often satirized in the literature of the century, as, for instance, in Addison's well known essay "The Dissection of the Beau's Head." No reader expects for a moment that he could possibly be a threat to the deep, mutual love of Fanny and Joseph.

In some confusion, Mrs. Adams apologized for the disorderly condition of her house, while her husband made bowing gestures and tried to overcome the awkwardness of the moment by showing off his son's ability in Latin. Lady Booby saw her opportunity here, and prevailed upon Adams to have the boy read to her (white Didapper occupied himself with Fanny, trying to subvert her affections).

CHAPTER 10

(This chapter, the story read by the boy, is a somewhat lengthy exemplum - Fielding calls it a "useful lesson to all those persons who happen to take up their residence in married families" - concerning two friends, one of whom [Paul] paid an extended visit to the other [Leonard], a man married to a woman who Paul had always thought to be of a most agreeable temper. They continually quarreled about trifles, however, and eventually appealed separately to Paul to confirm the righteousness of their positions. By assuring each in turn that he [and she] were in the right, but counseling them to yield the argument as a mark of marital affection, he managed to cause these disputes to become less frequent. Eventually, by bringing them closer to each other, he put himself out of favor and found his friendship with Leonard irrevocably severed. Here the story breaks off.)

Comment

It is difficult to see the relevance of this interpolated story, except for the fact that the relationship of Adams and his wife, and the future relationship of Joseph and Fanny are now of central importance in the narrative.

CHAPTER 11

The lad's story was interrupted by a sound box on the ear which Joseph administered to Didapper, when he saw him offer a rudeness to Fanny with his hands. The beau drew his sword, Adams interposed a potlid as a shield, and Joseph grasped his cudgel firmly. Mr. Booby, however, by promising Didapper that he should later have satisfaction, brought about a temporary peace, during which all of Lady Booby's party vehemently chided Joseph for taking the part of (and intending to marry) such a low-bred wench. Even Adams' wife and daughter joined the fray, with accusations against the parson of imprudence for offering his hospitality to Fanny and taking bread from his children's mouths. Only little Dick, the youngest, took Fanny's part and declared she was handsomer than any of his sisters. When Adams rebuked his wife for not remembering that Scripture asserts "that the husband is the head of the wife, and she is to submit and obey," she merely scoffed and told him to keep his preaching for Sundays. The Booby party having left, Joseph invited all the rest to a dinner at his expense at the George (an alehouse in the parish).

CHAPTER 12

The peddler, who had rescued young Dick from a drowning (the same peddler who had earlier relieved Joseph and Adams with his generosity) suddenly grew very inquisitive about the circumstances of Fanny's adoption by the Booby family. Acquainted with the facts, he announced that he could clear up the mystery of her parentage. While a drummer in an Irish regiment, he married (in common law) a woman he had met on the road near Bristol. On her deathbed she had revealed to him the only sin which lay heavy on her heart-she had, years before while travelling with a company of gypsies, stolen a beautiful young girl and later sold her to Sir Thomas Booby in Somersetshire. The child had been stolen from a family named Andrews.

Comment

This bombshell means, of course, that Fanny is in reality the sister of Joseph (and of Pamela), and that marriage with his is impossible. Incest, intentional or accidental, is frequent enough in high tragedy (as in *Oedipus the King* and *Hamlet);* here, we have a comic version of the incest them (as also in *Tom Jones*). Fanny fainted, Joseph turned pale, Dicky roared, and Adams fell on his knees to thank God that the discovery was made before the dreadful sin of incest was committed.

CHAPTER 13

Lady Booby, back in her chamber, was once more in the throes of rage, love, and despair, and (as if she enjoyed the agonies of her taunts) had sent for Slipslop, ordering her to do all she could to assist Didapper in his design of abducting Fanny. Slipslop was back in an instant, however, with the news that a strange man had disclosed the fact that Joseph and Fanny were brother and sister. Incredulous at first, and continuing to suspect the falsehood of the report from her earnest desire to believe it true, her ladyship nevertheless sent for Joseph, Fanny, and the parson, who were then seated in company with Mr. Booby, Didapper, Pamela, and herself. Joseph had been prevailed upon to ask the beau's pardon, and Adams and Didapper exchanged quips, while Pamela rebuked her brother for his sullenness at the turn events had taken. Adams then made it the occasion for a discourse on Platonic love and the theory that no true and lasting pleasure was to be found in this world. All then repaired to the separate beds which had been provided for them in the house.

CHAPTER 14

Sometime after three in the morning, Didapper, whose passion for Fanny had not cooled, betook himself (as he thought) to her bedroom, whispered sweet persuasions in her ear and climbed into bed. Shortly discovering that he had made the hideous error of entering the apartment of Slipslop, he tried to retreat without any uproar; but Slipslop, who saw this as an opportunity of publicly announcing her virtue, set up a hue and cry of rape. Instantly, Adams bounded into the room (entirely naked) and mistaking Didapper for the young maiden and Slipslop for the ravisher began to pummel Slipslop, imagining, from the shape he encountered, that it must be the Devil himself. Lady Booby arrived with a candle at this moment, and though highly amused at the scene, allowed Adams to depart to his own room. By making a wrong turn, that unhappy gentleman this time entered all unawares the bed of Fanny and fell promptly asleep until morning. Fanny, upon awakening, screamed for Joseph, who made some accusations against the parson. Adams finally persuaded them of his innocence, and left for his own chamber, asserting that he believed in the power of witchcraft, and did not see how a Christian could deny it.

Comment

It should be noted that the "adventures in this chapter are far more comic and far less painful than any Adams has undergone on the high road. This is a **foreshadowing**, and a fitting anticipation of the happy ending which will ensue.

CHAPTER 15

Gaffer and Gammer Andrews arrived at Booby Hall, and were made acquainted with the presence of Fanny and the peddler's story of her identity. Mrs. Andrews, embracing Fanny warmly, admitted that she was indeed her own daughter, born while her husband was away on a military campaign, and stolen by gypsies before he ever returned. Joseph, whom he imagined to be his natural son, was in fact a sickly child left by the gypsies in place of the girl they had abducted. The peddler confirmed all details which he had knowledge of, including the matter of the strawberry mark, at the mention of which Adams started up with a vague recollection of a story he had heard. Before he could say another word, however, he was notified that Mr. Wilson, who had promised to pay him a visit someday, was in fact at the door that very moment. At the mere mention of the word "strawberry" Wilson rushed in and embraced Joseph, who, when he was satisfied that he was indeed Wilson's son, embraced his father with tears and begged his blessing. (Lady Booby left the room in an agony.)

CHAPTER 16

Mr. Booby, with an extraordinary show of good nature, invited the entire party to his house for the wedding and celebration. At their first arrival the company "were all received by him in the most courteous and entertained in the most splendid manner, after the custom of the old English hospitality, which is still preserved in some very few families in the remote parts of England."

Comment

Fielding obviously places a very high valuation on the way of life of "merry old England," probably regarding Richardson's novel as the epitome of all the worst aspects of a rising mercantile society. Open-heartedness, good nature, and uncompromising morality-these are the qualities to be opposed to the scheming, calculating advocates of the quid pro quo to be found in Richardson's pages.

Mrs. Wilson was sent for and arrived on Saturday night. On Monday, the wedding took place as scheduled, Mr. Adams performing the ceremony. Joseph was dressed in a plain suit, and Fanny in nothing richer than a white dimity nightgown. Returning to Mr. Booby's house, the guests passed a day "with the utmost merriment, corrected by the strictest decency," after which Joseph and Fanny were free "to enjoy the private rewards of their constancy."

Joseph and Fanny returned to Mr. Wilson's parish, where they laid out an estate with the gift of two thousand pounds generously given to Fanny by Mr. Booby. Adams (though with some reluctance at leaving his old friends) accepted the living in Booby's parish of one hundred and thirty pounds a year. The peddler received handsome presents, and was given the post of exciseman, while Lady Booby returned to London, where a young captain of dragoons, and eternal card parties, soon obliterated the memory of Joseph. Joseph and Fanny lived on in the utmost mutual tenderness.

SUMMARY (CHAPTERS 9-16)

These final chapters contain all the surprising twists and turns of plot necessary to a pyrotechnic theatrical ending. Lady Booby's frantic efforts to prevent the marriage (including the engagement of Beau Didapper to bring about an estrangement between Fanny and Joseph) are constantly thwarted by quirks of fate. As for character, the integrity of Adams, the maturity of Joseph, the tender affections which bind the two lovers, and the absolute vanity of the leisured beaus, belles, toasts, and pimps of the aristocratic underworld of London are made to shine forth in a clear, uncompromising light. Goodness is suitably rewarded (the marriage of the lovers, the living bestowed on Adams, the presents and position awarded to the peddler) and vanity is left to create its own mundane hell, a pregnant picture of which was earlier provided in Wilson's account of his life.

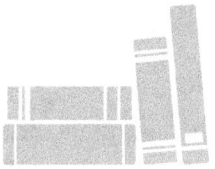

JOSEPH ANDREWS

CHARACTER ANALYSES

(There are over seventy characters who have some role to play, however insignificant, in the action of the novel, and a good two dozen more whose presence is alluded to. The fact that many of these are not named makes it difficult to distinguish them. There are, for instance, at least six innkeepers, only one of whom (Mr. Tow-wouse) is dignified with a name. The following analysis of selected characters omits those of minor importance and divides the remainder into: (a) Characters who participate significantly in the main plot of the novel, and (b) Characters who are included as exemplary figures of particular varieties of virtue or vice-these are mainly persons encountered by Adams on the high road and in the inns between London and Booby Hall; they may be said to be related to the **theme** rather than the plot.)

CHARACTERS OF THE PLOT

Joseph Andrews

Joseph is a footman in the service of the Booby family, a chaste young man who, as the novel begins, is the object of an attempted seduction by Lady Booby, shortly after the death of her husband. Dismissed for his lack of complaisance, Joseph returns to his village, encountering on the way his old friend Parson Adams, and his beloved Fanny Goodwill. He possesses manliness and uncompromising integrity, though in the beginning he is somewhat too much under the influence of Adams. He gains in forthrightness, however, becoming more mature and independent towards the end. He protects Fanny by fighting off bullies and would-be seducers, resists efforts to persuade him (when he is revealed to be a gentleman by birth) to reject Fanny and marry someone of higher station, and ends by marrying his beloved and setting up a small country estate with her, where they live in idyllic contentment.

Abraham Adams

Adams is the curate in the parish connected with Booby Hall. He is learned in the Latin and Greek tongues (carries a copy of *Aeschylus* with him always), has adopted a combination of classical stoicism and Christian charity and resignation to the will of God as his guide to life, and, while essentially a humble man, has a (very minor) blend of vanity and pugnaciousness which brings him into conflict with people he meets. Withal, he is an admirable individual-generous, fair, and true. He is on his way to London to sell his sermons when he meets Joseph and returns with him, encountering on the journey an incredible succession of knaves and hypocrites whom he is incapable of seeing through until they have done him an obvious evil turn.

Lady Booby

A sensual, morally depraved, designing woman, who attempts to seduce Joseph, and dismisses him when her vanity is insulted by his refusal. Her only qualm about an alliance with him is the fact that he is beneath her socially. She in vain, hypocritical, and unscrupulous; through her machinations Joseph and Fanny are almost sent to prison, and Fanny nearly becomes the victim of her agent, Beau Didapper.

Mrs. Slipslop

She is Lady Booby's waiting-gentlewoman, an affecter of "hard words" (which she invariably mangles-she may have been the prototype for Sheridan's famous Mrs. Malaprop). Slipslop, because she was the daughter of a country curate, fancies herself on her gentility. She is not a virgin (because of one slip in her youth) but, because of her repulsiveness, has never been attractive to men. She thinks her enforced chastity should be rewarded before it is too late, and she (like Lady Booby) wishes to seduce Joseph.

Peter Pounce

Lady Booby's steward (an "unjust steward"). By usury, chicanery, and gouging Pounce has amassed a small fortune. He cries "poor mouth" when he believes he may be touched for a loan, but brags about his wealth when he feels his eminence is being slighted. He is absolutely lacking in charity.

Fanny Goodwill

A beautiful country girl, simple in her affections and emotions, absolutely loyal to Joseph, whom she loves. She has set out on the dangerous journey to London to find him, and narrowly escapes being ravished a number of times.

Squire Booby

Lady Booby's nephew is borrowed by Fielding from Richardson's *Pamela,* in which he is an unscrupulous master who tries (unsuccessfully) by every means to seduce his servant Pamela, whom he eventually marries. In this book he is a rather kind, good-natured individual, who once gets Adams out of a jam, and then rescues Joseph and Fanny from the tender mercies of Justice Frolick. The marriage reception is held at his house and he has gifts for all deserving parties.

Pamela

(See above) In this book she is a moderately pleasant young woman who no longer speaks interminably about her "vartue" (as in Richardson's book), but has begun to put on a few airs as Mrs. Booby.

Mr. Wilson

As it turns out, of course, he is really Joseph's father. He was well educated, but lived the life of a rake and profligate for a long time, ruining a number of ladies and eventually impoverishing himself. Through the good offices of Harriet Hearty (who became his wife) he reformed and turned to the life of a retired country gentleman, his chief regret in life being for the loss of a young son, stolen by gypsies (Joseph-who is finally restored to him).

Lawyer Scout

He is a contemptible parasite of Lady Booby's untrained in the law, and capable of anything, including perjury, to gain his ends.

A Peddler

The unnamed peddler, who was formerly a drummer in an Irish regiment, has an importance beyond the amount of attention he receives. He is charitable, having given his last shilling to Adams to pay his bill; he saves Adams' son from drowning; and he reveals the business about Joseph's abduction by gypsies (since his wife, who had traveled with gypsies, made a deathbed confession of the theft). He is rewarded by Booby with the post of exciseman.

EXEMPLARY FIGURES

Betty

A chambermaid at the Dragon inn. Conventional morality is not her strong point (she thinks nothing of going to bed with Tow-wouse, for instance), but she has a heart of gold, and takes care of Joseph when he has been beaten and robbed.

Mrs. Tow-Wouse

Hostess at the Dragon. She is mean, nasty, uncharitable-a perfect shrew.

A Surgeon

He is a windy old fool, who uses his technical jargon to impress people. Typical satirical figure of the venal, pompous doctor.

Parson Barnabas

A stupid, ineffectual clergyman. He is an example of the "faith rather than good works" school, which Fielding abhorred.

A Bookseller

He is innocuous enough, but an example of the tough-minded, practical man of affairs whose point of view is diametrically opposed to that of Adams.

Mrs. Graveairs

An affected lady of fashion, who refuses to allow Joseph (a common footman) to ride in the same coach with her-the more ironic, because her family is nouveau riche.

The Italian Traveller

An English gentleman who has made a trip to Italy and returned with all the continual affectations. He spices his conversation with Italian terms, and pretends to despise the crudity of his countrymen.

The Man Of Courage

A gentleman whom Adams comes upon shooting partridges. All his talk is about the necessity for courage, and he criticizes the army for its lax conduct of a recent campaign. When he and Adams hear shouts of someone being attacked, he runs.

Parson Trulliber

A gross mountain of a man, parson on Sundays and hog-raiser on weekdays. He refuses to lend Adams money to pay a bill. He is a quoter of Scripture, but utterly lacking in charity (another of Fielding's major peeves).

A Mendacious Gentleman

Adams encounters a squire who is amiable in the extreme, professes great admiration and affection for Adams, and promises him a living, money for his bill, and passage home. But he disappears, and the innkeeper tells Adams that he has done this countless times. He seems to be an example of "good nature" in a specious form.

A Practical-Joking Squire

Sets his dogs on Adams and Joseph, then invites them to his home, where he "roasts" (that is, makes a mockery of) Adams, with the aid of his sycophantic followers, all of whom are grotesques of one sort or another.

Beau Didapper

He is the beau par excellence in the book. He is vain; weak, obnoxious, and fawning. Makes a halfhearted effort to attack Fanny on one occasion, tries to seduce her in front of Joseph on another and is soundly beaten for his pains.

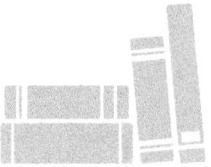

JOSEPH ANDREWS

CRITICAL COMMENTARY

EARLY RECEPTION

Joseph Andrews, when it first appeared in 1742, enjoyed a measure of popular success but did not evoke nearly as much interest as Richardson's *Pamela,* and comments by contemporaries of literary distinction are few. We do have, however, the interesting reactions of the poet Thomas Gray and his friend Richard West. On the whole, Gray did not care for the book, and although he allowed that "the characters have a great deal of nature" he thought "the incidents ill laid and without invention." West, who had recommended the book to Gray, chided him gently for his preference for the fantasies of the French sentimental writers over the **realism** of Fielding. Lady Mary Wortley Montagu, who did not come to the book until after she had read *Tom Jones,* said, after staying up all night to read it that she thought it superior to *Tom Jones.* And Hogarth himself, whom Fielding had complimented in his book, later recommended Fielding's Preface to the work for an explanation of the difference between character and caricature. For the most part, however, it attracted little favorable notice in the early years following its publication.

NINETEENTH CENTURY

The nineteenth century saw no full scale appreciations of Fielding, though there was a constant enthusiasm for *Joseph Andrews* among the bright literary lights, especially for his triumph in creating Parson Adams. Lamb thought an appreciation of Parson Adams a touchstone for literary taste, and Coledridge (who preferred Fielding infinitely to Richardson) declared it impossible to rise from a reading of *Joseph Andrews* without having been made a better man for it. Sir Walter Scott also thought Fielding's accomplishment in creating Adams an absolute testimony of his greatness, an opinion echoed by Leigh Hunt. With the Victorians Fielding fared less well. Thackeray, who admired his work and thought "honest Joseph Andrews" the finest of Fielding's heroes, was partly responsible also for the popular picture of the author as a confirmed rake; this opinion, aided by a growing sentiment in favor of romantic plots and settings, caused Fielding's star to decline.

MODERN CRITICAL OPINION

Real understanding of Fielding's accomplishment in *Joseph Andrews* was forthcoming only in our own century. Wilbur L. Cross's voluminous *History of Henry Fielding* (1918) praises him for narrative fluency - "Through all the varied scenes of the road the narrative glides without friction, as if it were nature itself" - and he describes Parson Adams as "one of the glories of human nature." The French critic Digeon (1925) speaks of the novel's "perfection of artistry," though he limits the importance of Joseph to the scale of Lady Booby-the function of both is merely "to carry the plot along." Adams is a "great figure" around whom "a whole world of secondary characters moves," the play between them, however, remaining marvelously supple. E. A. Baker, in his authoritative *History of the English Novel* (1930), calls "the illusion that [Fielding] achieved . . . unprecedented in its completeness [and] perfect verisimilitude."

There has probably been more searching, analytical criticism of *Joseph Andrews* in the past twenty years than in all the years since its publication. Maynard Mack's introduction to the Rinehart edition (1948) is a notable beginning. He speaks of Adams as "an unusually effective instrument of social criticism," declaring that "his education in the world's ways is to a large extent a criticism of them by a higher standard. . . . Thus in a sense his career can be looked on as a parable of the eighteenth-century conscience uncovering some realities to which it has been blind." Mack is one of the first to attempt a definition of the structure of the novel, alleging that Fielding uses structure, as a playwright does, to articulate his **theme**. The two poles of value in *Joseph Andrews* . . . are the country-world and the city, neither perfect, but the former superior to the latter because more honest." Arnold Kettle (1951) speaks of the structure of the novel ton, but declares that it derives from the form of the journey, and adds: "In so far as in the journey certain moral discoveries are involved the journey does itself symbolize a striving for clarity; the rhythms of the journey . . . hint at the rhythms of life itself." Fielding's pervading sense is one of "generous humanity," springing from "a very explicit social awareness and understanding of the people." The novel has been attacked (by Digeon for one) for its contrived ending. Spilka (1953) defends it from this charge by pointing out that the hilarious night-time escapades at Booby Hall are a "comic resolution" of the major themes. John Butt (1954) sees in the novel the basic pattern of an "Odysseyan epic," in which it is "the hatred of Venus [Lady Booby] rather than the wrath of Poseidon that supplies the Cause of the action." The great end of the work is "the display of the Ridiculous, of those affectations which arise from vanity and hypocrisy." McKillop (1956) similarly identifies the **theme** of the book as "social maladjustment caused by the deviations of individuals from a norm of rational morality," but stresses the importance of the narrative persona, claiming that he "imparts to the story a higher unity than is derived from the mechanism of the plot."

M. C. Battestin's book, *The Moral Basis of Fielding's Art,* is the only book-length study of *Joseph Andrews.* After several chapters in which he establishes with a wealth of contemporary reference the background of religious controversy (strict Methodism vs. latitudinarianism, for example), the current idea of the Christian hero, and the prevailing climate of ethical opinion, Battestin turns to the meaning and structure of the novel; relying heavily on an analysis of the autobiographical story told by Wilson as a dramatization of "Fielding's recurrent insistence upon the operation of Providence and the moral responsibility of the individual," he concludes that "the broad allegory of the novel represents the pilgrimage of Joseph Andrews and Abraham Adams-like their scriptural namesakes, Christian heroes exemplifying the essential virtues of the good man-from the vanity of the town to the relative naturalness and simplicity of the country." Study of the novel continues in articles in learned journals, a recent example of which is Taylor's essay emphasizing the growth in independence and maturity which Joseph's character undergoes, and thus redressing a balance which gave Adams a position of unquestioned centrality. Critical discussion of the characterization, unity, and moral seriousness of the novel will unquestionably continue for a long time.

JOSEPH ANDREWS

ESSAY QUESTIONS AND ANSWERS

Question: Does Fielding's frequent use of accident (chance meetings, opportune arrivals, exchange of infants, and so forth) mar his effectiveness as a story-teller?

Answer: It is a grim reader indeed who looks for absolute verisimilitude in *Joseph Andrews*. For one thing, Fielding is at pains constantly to keep his readers aware that the manipulation of his characters is in his own control. As he makes clear in the Preface to Book III, he is concerned not with the truth of fact but with faithfulness to human nature. The central instance of this conception is perhaps the role played by the peddler. His encounter with Adams is entirely fortuitous, and yet his role is absolutely essential to the evolution of the plot. Fielding needs his intervention to make clear certain facts about the abduction of Joseph (as well as Fanny) by marauding bands of gypsies, but what is true about his actions is that they are the result of a good nature such as we expect to find in a man of his circumstances. Having once made charitable overtures to Adams in a wayside inn, there is nothing unnatural or unexpected about his later acts of virtue - rescuing young Dick from the river, and revealing the true circumstances of Joseph's early life. Like the postilion who gave Joseph his coat, and Betty the chambermaid who nursed him, the impecunious peddler acts just as our previous experience with indigent but charitable individuals makes us believe he will act. Thus, once we admit the likelihood of the first chance encounter the rest seems inevitable.

Question: Is Fielding's alleged moral purpose at all vitiated by his occasionally frank sensuousness of description?

Answer: To begin with, a comparison with Richardson's book would be helpful. In his professedly moral work there is more descriptive lubricity by far than one finds in Fielding. When Pamela is brought to bed between Mrs. Jewkes and Mr. Booby, for example, Richardson's superficial horror cannot conceal a certain lickerish interest in physical detail. This is not Fielding's way at all. Even the scene in which Lady Booby has Joseph visit her in her room is unexceptionable in its modesty of description. There are perhaps three scenes in which some frankness is to be noted, and these may be treated in order. Tow-wouse's assignation with Betty the chambermaid is described in such an abstract and roundabout way that there is hardly a suggestion of physical contact. The nocturnal misadventure of Beau Didapper in Slipslop's bed (he thinks it is Fanny's), and Adam's gallant (though naked) charge into the room, with all the attendant jostling and tearing of clothes, is so hilarious that it is difficult to take any of it seriously. There are scenes, especially toward the close of the book, in which kisses and embraces (in one case, Joseph's prolonged staring at Fanny) are described quite bluntly. But this is precisely the point. Fielding offers these in a totally unembarrassed fashion as a challenge to his readers to find them objectionable. When one has done with all the Didappers and the other would-be ravishers along the high road, he must still face the fact that the pure love of Joseph and Fanny has its physical side too. The real point is that chastity and sensual pleasure are not mutually exclusive.

Question: Do the author's frequent intrusions into the narrative in his own person (to supply information, for instance, that he believes his reader should have, or to discourse on his theories of art) destroy the illusion of reality that we usually expect from a work of fiction?

Answer: We must always remember, of course, that the illusion of reality in fiction, like the **convention** of the audience as a "fourth wall" in the theater, is a comparatively late development. In fiction, the passion for an absolute faithfulness to a limited point of view probably goes back no farther than Henry James. Fielding, to be sure, goes even beyond the device of the "omniscient observer," since he forecasts actions, applauds or criticizes his own techniques, and even makes occasions for discursive essays on ideas suggested to him by the action. His age was, for one thing, more relaxed in its notions of organic unity in literature than our own, and, for another, an age which placed a high valuation on conversational ease as a social accomplishment. In one sense, Fielding is a gentleman in his drawing room, entertaining his friends with a leisurely narrative which leaves many opportunities for divagations on subjects of mutual interest. (The vestiges of this tradition may be noted in Conrad's use of Marlow as his narrator, with the occasional asides that he permits him.) Rather than a blot on the structure of the work, Fielding's personal intrusions add to the charm of the journey.

Question: Comment on Fielding's artistic use of juxtaposition and analogy.

Answer: There are a number of **episodes** in the book which interrupt or slow up the narrative, and which are generally referred to as "interpolated" stories. The story of the "Unfortunate Jilt" (Leonora and Bellarmine), and Wilson's account of his life in London are two of the more important of these, to which we may add the song sung by Joseph, which is overheard by Fanny and Adams, and leads to their reunion. There is now rather general critical agreement that Fielding intended these to stand in a symbolic or analogous relationship to the main action, or to serve some functional purpose. The Leonora story, for one thing, is an example of the sort of sentimental, fashionable narrative (like *Pamela*) the limited sensibility of which is being criticized by Fielding. Moreover, since it involves a love affair between a calculating modish lady and an affected beau, it serves to comment on the simple, unabashed emotions of Joseph and Fanny, as well as to underscore the **theme** of the prevalence of vanity and hypocrisy in all walks of life. Wilson's account of his dissolute life in London is a way of creating a picture of corrupt London society, without the necessity of having Adams himself make the journey there. It is the sharpest focusing, also, of the **theme** (mentioned by Maynard Mack) of the polarity between the two ways of life, with the life of rural solitude emerging as the positive pole. The song sung by Joseph has a similar function. By being a cliche-ridden love **ballad**, which, in a sudden change of tone, deals with the consummation of a love, it emphasizes the difference between the kind of love which a virile though chaste young man of Joseph's stamp is capable of, compared, for instance, to the conventionalized maunderings of the almost epicene Beau Didapper.

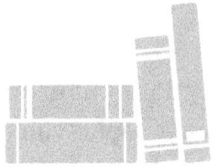

JOSEPH ANDREWS

SUBJECT BIBLIOGRAPHY AND GUIDE TO RESEARCH PAPERS

EDITIONS

The Complete Works of Henry Fielding, Esq., ed. William Ernest Henley et al., 16 vols., London, 1903.

The Adventures of Joseph Andrews, ed. J. Paul de Castro, London, 1929.

Joseph Andrews, ed. Maynard Mack, New York (*Rinehart Editions*), 1948.

Joseph Andrews and Shamela, ed. Martin C. Battestin, Boston (Riverside Editions), 1961.

BIOGRAPHIES AND FULL-LENGTH STUDIES

Banerji, H. K. *Henry Fielding: Playwright, Journalist, and Master of the Art of Fiction*, Oxford, 1929.

Butt, John. *Fielding (Writers and Their Work, No. 57)*, London, 1954.

Blanchard, Frederic T. *Fielding the Novelist: A Study in Historical Criticism,* New Haven, 1927.

Cross, Wilbur L. *The History of Henry Fielding*, New Haven, 1918.

Dudden, F. Homes. *Henry Fielding: His Life, Work, and Times,* Oxford, 1952.

Digeon, Aurelien. *The Novels of Fielding* (Eng. trans.), London, 1925.

Jenkins, Elizabeth. *Henry Fielding*, Denver, Colorado, 1948.

Johnson, Maurice. *Fielding's Art of Fiction*, Philadelphia, 1961.

Jones, Benjamin M. *Henry Fielding, Novelist and Magistrate,* London, 1933.

Thornbury, Ethel. *Henry Fielding's Theory of the Comic Prose Epic,* Madison, 1931.

BOOKS ON JOSEPH ANDREWS

Battestin, Martin C. *The Moral Basis of Fielding's Art: A Study of Joseph Andrews,* Middletown, Connecticut, 1959.

STUDIES OF THE ENGLISH NOVEL, CONTAINING STUDIES OF FIELDING

Baker, Ernest A. *The History of the English Novel*, London, 1930 (Vol. 4).

Kettle, Arnold. *An Introduction to the English Novel*, London, 1951 (Vol. 1).

McKillop, A. D. *The Early Masters of English Fiction,* Lawrence, Kansas, 1956 (Pp. 98-146, "Henry Fielding").

Watt, Ian. *The Rise of the Novel: Studies in Defoe, Richardson, and Fielding,* London, 1957.

ARTICLES

Baker, Sheridan. "Henry Fielding's Comic Romances," *Papers of the Michigan Academy of Sciences, Arts, and Letters,* XLV (1960).

Battestin, Martin C. "Fielding's Changing Politics and *Joseph Andrews,*" *Philological Quarterly,* XXXIX (1960).

Cauthen, I. B., Jr. "Fielding's Digressions in *Joseph Andrews,*" *College English,* XVII (1956).

Ehrenpreis, Irvin. "Fielding's Use of Fiction: The Autonomy of *Joseph Andrews,*" in *Twelve Original Essays on Great English Novels,* Detroit, 1960.

Mack, Maynard. "Introduction [to *Joseph Andrews*]," in *Rinehart Edition,* New York, 1948.

Spilka, Mark. "Comic Resolution in Fielding's *Joseph Andrews,*" *College English,* XV (1953).

Sherburn, George. "Fielding's Social Outlook," *Philological Quarterly,* XXXV (1956).

Taylor, Dick, Jr. "Joseph as Hero in *Joseph Andrews,*" *Tulane Studies in English,* VII (1957).

Wallace, Robert M. "Fielding's Knowledge of History and Biography," *Studies in Philology,* XLIV (1947).

Woods, Charles B. "Fielding and the Authorship of *Shamela*," *Philological Quarterly*, XXV (1946).

Work, James A. "Henry Fielding, Christian Censor," in *The Age of Johnson: Essays Presented to Chauncey Brewster Tinker*, New Haven, 1949.

TOPICS FOR RESEARCH AND CRITICAL ANALYSIS

1. Fielding's debt to and modification of earlier literary traditions:

    a. The picaresque novel: For comparison and analysis, read an English picaresque novel, Thomas Nashe's *The Unfortunate Traveller* for instance, and compare it with *Joseph Andrews* from the standpoint of unity of theme, seriousness of purpose, and adequacy of characterization.

    b. The "mirror of fools" tradition: *Joseph Andrews* is, in part, a catalogue of the knaves and fools to be found dispersed along the high road in England. Read one or more of the following to discover what, in Fielding's observations of vicious and foolish characters, has perennial validity: Nigel Longchamp's *A Mirror for Fools* (13th c., trans. J. H. Mozley); Chaucer, *The Canterbury Tales*; Desiderius Erasmus, *The Praise of Folly;* Sebastian Brant, *The Ship of Fools* (trans, Edwin Zeydel).

    c. The "comedy of humors": Which of the characters in *Joseph Andrews* are "humorous" in the Jonsonian sense? Compare Fielding's method of depicting humorous characters with some of Jonson's characterizations in *Volpone, The Alchemist*, or *Every Man in His Humour*.

    d. The periodical essay: How many passages in *Joseph Andrews* (such as the disquisition on "high people" and "low people" in II, 13) might stand alone as essays of the sort to be found in the *Spectator of Addison and Steel*, or Johnson's *Rambler?* How do they compare in style and structure with the periodical essays you are familiar with? How consistent are they with the persona established by Fielding as his narrative and expository voice? How relevant are they to the main **theme** and plot of the novel, and how well integrated?

2. Examine one or more of the "interpolated" stories (the Leonora and Bellarmine story, Wilson's account of his life, and young Dick's tale of the two friends Leonard and Paul). In what way, and how successfully, is each related to the main story? Are any of them symbolic (that is, do they stand in a relationship of analogy to some phase of the main action)?

3. In what way do the names Joseph and Abraham (even, perhaps, Adam), by suggesting the stories of their Biblical prototypes, create an allegorical level in the novel? This analysis might also be a basis for a lengthier comparison between Bunyan (his allegorical Pilgrim's Progress) and Fielding as moral allegorists.

4. Read Samuel Richardson's *Pamela: Or Virtue Rewarded*, and write an essay commenting on the aptness of Coleridge's remark that reading Fielding after Richardson

"is like emerging from a sickroom into the light of a sunshiny day." Make whatever other comparisons suggest themselves in the two authors' handling of style, characterization, moral evaluation, and so forth. A reading of Fielding's *Shamela*–an outright **parody** of *Pamela*-might be provocative of further ideas.

5. Read one or more of Fielding's early plays, and analyze the influence of dramaturgical practice on the composition of *Joseph Andrews*. What resemblances in structure may be seen? In characterization? Does the author seem more at home with the drama or the novel?

6. Select three or four major characters other than *Joseph and Adams*, and examine the relationship Fielding establishes between their physical appearance and their characters. Are physical details, mannerisms, gestures, idiosyncrasies of speech, related to their moral natures as these are determined by the actions they perform?

7. Discuss the picture of the law and lawyers we find in *Joseph Andrews* in the light of Fielding's own juridical experience (see Wilbur L. Cross's *The History of Henry Fielding* for biographical data).

8. By reviewing the attitudes of a number of major characters towards the concepts of charity, good nature, and virtue, attempt to define Fielding's understanding of these terms. Do the following characters possess charity: Squire Booby? Mrs. Adams? Tow-wouse? Is Mr. Wilson a goodnatured man? Discuss (with reasons) the ways in which the following characters lack these three qualities: Mrs. Tow-wouse; Parson Trulliber; Lawyer Scout.

9. Discuss the opposition between London life and country life as a structural principle in the book. What are the baneful effects of living in the city according to Fielding? (A comparison with Johnson's poem *The Vanity of Human Wishes* might be helpful here.) Exactly what aspects of life in the country have an influence for good? How are human passions affected by rural peace and beauty?

10. Who is the "hero" of the novel, Joseph Andrews or Abraham Adams. Discuss in detail.

11. One of the central critical issues in recent discussion of *Joseph Andrews* is the question of structural unity. Do you think the action centering about Lady Booby's intrigue (her attempted seduction of Joseph) is successfully integrated with the action centering around the journey of Joseph and Adams back to their village? (This answer could easily be expanded into a lengthy paper by a comparison of *Joseph Andrews* with Homer's *Odyssey* and Cervantes' *Don Quixote* on the matter of total design tending to express a single significant **theme**. What is the theme of *Joseph Andrews?*)

12. The theological and philosophical controversies of the first half of the eighteenth century are very much Fielding's concern in this book (see Martin C. Battestin, *The Moral Basis of Fielding's Art*). Depending, of course, on availability of source material, a detailed study might be made of one of the following subjects:

    a) The influence of sermon literature on Fielding's style and structure.

b) Fielding's position with respect to the theories of Hobbes, Mandeville, or Shaftesbury.

c) The extent of Fielding's latitudinarianism.

13. Investigate Fielding's political opinions (in his essays and other non-fiction) and his relations with the Walpole government, and consider the possibility of political **allusions** in *Joseph Andrews.*

14. Is *Tom Jones* clearly superior to *Joseph Andrews* in all respects? How do they compare in structure? Characterization? The nature of the hero.

15. Consider the question of characterization in Fielding's prose and Hogarth's illustrations (see Cross, History, for biographical details, and information about their acquaintance and respect for each other's work).

www.ingramcontent.com/pod-product-compliance
Lightning Source LLC
LaVergne TN
LVHW011720060526
838200LV00051B/2968